Peter And The Children

66 Puppet Talks

H. Burnham Kirkland

CSS Publishing Company, Inc., Lima, Ohio

PETER AND THE CHILDREN

Copyright © 2004 by
CSS Publishing Company, Inc.
Lima, Ohio

For more information about CSS Publishing Company resources, visit our website at www.csspub.com or e-mail us at custserv@csspub.com or call (800) 241-4056.

ISBN: 978-0-7880-2300-2

PRINTED IN U.S.A.

This book is dedicated
to
Margaret and Miller Wachs
who brought Peter into my life
and to
all the children and adults
who found joy and inspiration
in knowing Peter.

Foreword

If you are interested in something different for your Sunday morning Children's Talks, this book is for you.

Some years ago I attended a Christian Education Workshop and was introduced to Puppet Ministry. I was particularly intrigued by the "rod puppet." This is a figure with jointed arms that are manipulated by rods attached to the wrists of the figure. The puppeteer inserts one arm inside the body of the puppet and controls the movement of the puppet's mouth and head with one hand, while moving the arms by means of the rods with the other.

A couple in my church presented me with a "rod puppet." I named him Peter, and it was upon this "rock" that I built my puppet ministry.

One does not have to be an expert, nor does one need to be a ventriloquist. You do have to develop a voice for the puppet that is somewhat different from your regular speaking voice. When Peter, the puppet, is speaking, the children are watching and listening to him and not wondering if your lips are moving.

The scripts in this book are intended for use with just the pastor and the puppet. This avoids the necessity of having a puppet stage and/or more than one puppeteer. These usually tend to disrupt the service, while simply having a dialogue between Peter (the puppet) and the Pastor presents no staging problems.

Variety can be obtained by changing the puppet's clothes in keeping with the season or the story, as well as by using other props. With a little imagination these can be attached to the puppet's hand or utilized in some other manner.

Puppets are not just another gimmick, but an important teaching tool. You will find that children listen carefully to the message presented by the puppet. Adults, too, will be attentive and absorb the lesson. Puppets add a bit of informality to the service without detracting from its sacredness.

Puppets are generally available through most Christian bookstores.

Don't be afraid to give it a try. I was amazed at how quickly "Peter" developed a personality, and the children as well as the adults fell in love with him.

H.B.K.

New Year's

Pastor: Good morning, Peter!

Peter: Good morning to you, Pastor. It is surely nice to be here this New Year's Sunday!

Pastor: Is that your basketball shirt you have on, Peter, with your player number?

Peter: Oh, no! That's my class shirt!

Pastor: I see. You graduated from kindergarten in 2002. So that puts you in the class of Zero Two or '02.

Peter: Well, you are partly right, but you didn't pronounce it correctly.

Pastor: Why? What's wrong with '02?

Peter: Because it should be "Ought to." My parents and my teachers keep telling me:
- I ought to study more;
- I ought to watch TV less;
- I ought to drink my milk;
- I ought to study my Sunday school lessons;
- I ought to help around the house;
- I ought to be careful of the company I keep (no insult intended) ...

Pastor: Well, I think I'm getting the idea. You are not in a class by yourself. There are a lot of things all of us *ought* to be doing, that we don't.

Peter: You'd better believe it; and remember the Bible tells us to number our days that we may get a heart of wisdom.

Pastor: And don't forget Paul's warning to "make the most of your time for these are evil days."

Peter: I remember that one because he goes on to say: "Don't get drunk with wine." That's a good word for kids in high school and college especially.

Pastor: And while we are remembering Bible verses, let's not forget the one in Ecclesiastes that says: "For everything there is a season and a time for every matter under heaven."

Peter: Boys and girls, young men and women, now is the time for us to build strong bodies and strong minds, to build a love of beauty, to learn to know and love God. Let's graduate from "OUGHT TO" to "WILL DO" this year. Have a good week, boys and girls, and Happy New Year to you.

Pastor: Let us pray together: Our heavenly Father, we thank you that we can come to you and be forgiven for all the things we ought to have done this past year but failed to do. Help us in this New Year you have given us to graduate from "OUGHT TO" to "WILL DO." Amen.

Buffet Sunday

Peter: Boy, did I ever have trouble getting you to church this morning. Boy, oh boy, I can hardly wait.

Pastor: What was the big hurry, Peter? It was only six o'clock and you wanted to go to church.

Peter: Well, I just wanted to get a good seat, so when they pass the food, I can get first in line.

Pastor: Pass out what food? They don't serve food in church!

Peter: Oh, yes, they do. This is Buffet Sunday, when it's okay to have crackers and juice in church. It's great fun. Boy, last time the little glass of grape juice they gave me hardly washed down the piece of bread. Stuck to my teeth terrible!

Pastor: Wait a minute. Bread, Juice. You mean Communion Sunday.

Peter: Sure, that's it. It must be important because look at the extra clergy up here.

Pastor: Peter, this happens to be a very special Sunday that represents a commitment of the Christians in the church.

Peter: What can be so important about a little bread and a shot of grape juice?

Pastor: It's not what they are — it's what they represent. The bread stands for Christ's body that was broken for sinners.

Peter: Really? What does the juice stand for?

13

Pastor: That stands for Christ's blood shed on the cross; and as often as we eat the bread and drink the juice, we show remembrance of Christ until he comes again.

Peter: Who said all those things?

Pastor: Jesus said them to his disciples on the night of the Last Supper.

Peter: Boy, I didn't realize that this Sunday was so important. From now on, I will never forget what Communion Sunday stands for.

Pastor: I'm glad you understand now about Communion. Next time don't get me up so early, and remember — there is always room at the Lord's table!

Let us pray: Lord, as we come to your table this morning, we give thanks that there is always room for everyone, and we praise your holy name that Jesus came to forgive us our sins. Amen.

Will Roast Pig Bring Us Luck?

Pastor: Good morning, boys and girls. Good morning, Peter! The other day I was reading in the encyclopedia about some unusual foods that people eat to celebrate the New Year.

Peter: That's right! Did you know that people in Japan eat a fish called carp? Carp are able to swim against strong currents and even leap waterfalls. So, as they eat carp, people hope that they, too, will be able to do difficult things in the coming year.

Pastor: It says, too, that people in Hungary eat roast pig with an apple or a four-leaf clover in its mouth and they hope for a lucky year.

Peter: That's nothing! In some lands people eat black-eyed peas to make them strong, chestnuts to bring them good luck, or even chicken gizzards to make them beautiful during the coming year.

Pastor: Of course, we know that eating carp won't ensure that we will be able to do difficult things in the coming year; and eating roast pig won't really bring us good luck, or black-eyed peas won't by themselves make us strong, or eating chestnuts won't bring us good luck, or eating chicken gizzards won't necessarily make us beautiful.

Peter: But there are some things that can make us strong and healthy. Lots of good exercise, eating the right kinds of foods, studying hard in school, and letting God be our friend and our partner in everything we do.

Pastor: That's good advice, Peter. Boys and girls, I hope you will remember that during the year. If you practice that good advice you will continue to grow strong in every way — mentally, physically, and spiritually!

Let us pray: Almighty God, our Friend and Partner in everything we do, help us to take care of our bodies, minds, and souls that we may grow into the kind of men and women you would have us to be. Amen.

Talk To The Shepherd

Pastor: Good morning, Peter!

Peter: Good morning, Pastor. One, two, three ...

Pastor: What are you counting, Peter?

Peter: Oh, I was just thinking about last night.

Pastor: What about last night?

Peter: Well, I stayed over at this friend's house, and I couldn't go to sleep. So, I started counting sheep, and my friend said I was weird.

Pastor: What sheep were you counting, Peter?

Peter: Oh, they weren't real sheep. They were in my mind.

Pastor: That is weird.

Peter: Didn't you ever hear of counting sheep? You know, when you can't sleep you think of sheep jumping over a fence, and you count them.

Pastor: How many sheep do you have to count?

Peter: Oh, sometimes just a few; and sometimes on a stormy night I have to count a couple hundred sheep.

Pastor: That is weird.

Peter: Okay, smarty! What do you do when you can't fall asleep?

Pastor: Well, I don't count sheep. I talk to the Shepherd.

Peter: You what?

Pastor: I talk to the Shepherd.

Peter: What shepherd? If my sheep are in my mind, where is your shepherd?

Pastor: The Bible says Jesus is the Shepherd and he watches over his flock; and I'm one of his flock.

Peter: Jesus is a shepherd?

Pastor: Yes, Jesus is the Good Shepherd, and when I can't sleep, or when I get scared, I talk to Jesus.

Peter: Wow!

Pastor: You don't have to be scared to talk to Jesus. Sometimes I just talk to him and say, "Thanks."

Peter: Thanks for what?

Pastor: Thanks for whatever — my family, my friends, my church, my Sunday school.

Peter: Say, that's neat! If Jesus is the Good Shepherd, then that explains this stuff on my t-shirt about the First Church Flock. That means we are all his sheep and he loves us.

Pastor: That's right, and as good sheep we need to *flock* together. We should be in Sunday school and church every Sunday.

Peter: Especially this month because it's Sunday School Rally Month!

Pastor: Well, boys and girls, you'd better be sure to come to Sunday school and bring your friends. Remember, you are God's little lambs and you need to *flock* together. Come to Sunday school and learn about Jesus, the Good Shepherd, and have a good time, too!

Peter: So long, boys and girls! I'll see you in Sunday school. And wear your shirt like mine if you have one. I love you — baa, baa!

Pastor: Let us pray: Lord Jesus, you are the Good Shepherd and we are your sheep. Watch over us and keep us from straying from the flock. Amen.

Scout Sunday

Pastor: Well, Peter, it is good to have you here this morning all dressed up in your scout uniform.

Peter: Oh, you noticed, did you? Bet you didn't know that I'm a member of Pack 515. I salute all you Den Mothers out there — past and present ... Pretty snappy, huh?

Pastor: Well, we do congratulate all the scouts for being part of a great organization. By the way, Peter, are you physically strong, mentally awake, and morally straight?

Peter: I'm strong all right, and you can be sure I'm straight, but I don't know about being awake.

Pastor: Well, let me test you: What is the middle of this week?

Peter: That's easy — Wednesday!

Pastor: Oh, I know that, but what's special about it?

Peter: I give up.

Pastor: It's the birthday of Abraham Lincoln. He was born about 200 years ago on February 12.

Peter: Oh, I know about "Honest Abe" — we learned about him in school.

Pastor: So you learned about President Lincoln's honesty in school. Well, here is something they may not teach in school anymore. When Lincoln was elected President and left his hometown to go to Washington, D.C., the last thing he said in a speech to his friends was this: "Without God's help, we cannot succeed. But with God's help, we cannot fail."

Peter: You mean Honest Abe Lincoln was able to do all that he did because he depended on God?

Pastor: That's right, and we can depend on God to lead us and to help us to know what to do and to have the courage to do it, every day, just as Abraham Lincoln did.

By the way, Peter, do you know what else we celebrate this week?

Peter: Of course. Everybody knows that February 14 is Valentine's Day.

Pastor: And what do we do on Valentine's Day?

Peter: We give valentines to the people we love — Mom, Dad, Brother, Sister, friends, teachers ... Have you made my valentine yet?

Pastor: A long time ago, in the days of Jesus, they didn't have paper and crayons. But they had lots of love.

Peter: I know ... one of my favorite Sunday school stories is the one about Jesus and how he loved the little children.

Pastor: That's right, Peter. Jesus loves all the children and grown-ups, too; so when we tell people we love them by sending them a valentine, we are also reminding them that Jesus loves them.

Peter: Boys and girls, I want you all to be my valentine because I love you and Jesus loves you, too.

Pastor: Boys and girls (and all the adults, too), let's sing our prayer as we sing together "Jesus Loves Me."

Scout Sunday II

Pastor: Hi, Peter! It's good to have you here this morning dressed up in your Scout uniform.

Peter: Oh, you noticed, did you? Bet you didn't know that I'm a member of Pack 515, and I have a great Den Mother. I salute you! Pretty snappy huh?

Pastor: Say, Peter, before we talk about today — do you know what next Wednesday is?

Peter: Oh, sure — some of my friends love that day. It's Ash Wednesday, and they don't have to wash their faces after they go to church.

Pastor: Well, I bet you don't know what next Tuesday is.

Peter: Sure, I do. It's the day before Ash Wednesday.

Pastor: I know that, but what is it called?

Peter: I don't know — do you?

Pastor: Do you think I would ask if I didn't? It is called Fat Tuesday and in some places it is a legal holiday.

Peter: Why do they call it Fat Tuesday?

Pastor: Well, in olden times Lent was a very solemn, serious time. So Mardi Gras was the last fling before Lent began, and Mardi Gras means Fat Tuesday.

Peter: That's all very interesting, but we're not celebrating Mardi Gras or Fat Tuesday today — we are celebrating Boy Scout Week!

Pastor: That's right, Peter, and I've got a Bible verse for the occasion.

Peter: You would — well, what is it?

Pastor: Jeremiah 31:21. It says: "Set up waymarks; make for yourself guideposts." In this verse, God is telling the prophet Jeremiah to make a trail for the people of Israel who had lost their way and needed to be guided back to God. You see, in those days they didn't have road maps or sign posts to tell the way. So they used stones and grass and trees.

Peter: Our scouts do the same today. If you go hiking and see some stones piled one on top of the other, you know you have found the trail. If you were walking in a meadow and came on a bunch of grass tied and bent in a certain direction, you would know a Scout has been that way. If you see a broken twig or branch shaped like an arrow, you'll know it is intended to point the way to go.

Pastor: Say, that's great, Peter. I'm glad to see you're learning so much. Tell me, are there any guideposts in the Bible?

Peter: Oh, sure — there are the Ten Commandments.

Pastor: Any other

Peter: Well, there are the Two Great Commandments.

Pastor: And what are they?

Peter: Oh, you know: Thou shalt love the Lord your God with all your mind, etc., etc., etc.; and you shall love your neighbor as yourself.

Pastor: Very good, Peter. So God is constantly saying in the Bible: This is the way — this is the path of life to follow. Unfortunately, people don't always obey the signals or pay attention to the guideposts.

Peter: I know — one day we were out on a hike, and some wise guy decided he wouldn't follow the Den Mother, and half the pack followed him down the wrong trail and ended up in a batch of poison ivy.

Pastor: Well, that's a good lesson. It is not always wise just to follow blindly — unless we are sure they are good people. By the way, Peter, what is the Scout motto?

Peter: "Be Prepared."

Pastor: That's right — and Jesus wants us always to Be Prepared to follow him — by keeping ourselves physically strong, mentally awake, and morally straight.

Peter: Try to remember that, boys and girls, and have a good week.

Camp Fire

Pastor: Good morning, Peter. We missed you on Girl Scout Sunday.

Peter: Well, I thought two of us would be more than you could handle.

Pastor: You're probably right.

Peter: Besides, I'm not a Girl Scout.

Pastor: What are you? I see your shirt says you're a "Spark." Does that mean you go around setting fires?

Peter: No, silly. I'm part of the Camp Fire USA Program.

Pastor: I thought that was just for girls — you know — "Camp-fire Girls."

Peter: Boy, that just shows how out-of-date you are. Today it is just called Camp Fire, and boys make up almost forty percent of the membership.

Pastor: Well, thanks for bringing me up to date. Now back to your "Spark."

Peter: Oh, that! That means I belong to the Kindergarten group. The next three grades are called Blue Birds. Then there is Adventure, Discovery, Horizon, and Aces.

Pastor: What do you do as Camp Fire members?

Peter: We have lots of fun. We go camping, do service projects, and learn new skills making things and playing games.

Pastor: What was that word I heard you muttering before church?

Peter: I wasn't muttering. I was saying our Camp Fire byword — WO-HE-LO. Wo-He-Lo. It has a nice ring to it, don't you think?

Pastor: Sure, but what does it mean?

Peter: Well, you take the first letters of three words: Work - Health - Love, and you get Wo-He-Lo.

Pastor: And those three words are very important.
   Work — we need to learn to glorify work.
   Health — we need to hold on to health.
   Love — we need to love one another.

Peter: You got it. Why don't you join Camp Fire?

Pastor: I'm a little old for that, but it is a great organization, and we are glad to have a chance to salute all you Camp Fire people.

Peter: Have a good week, boys and girls — and remember our byword: Wo-He-Lo. Glorify Work; Hold on to Health; and Love one another.

Anniversary Sunday

Pastor: Good morning, boys and girls. Good morning to you, too, Peter.

Peter: Good morning! This is a very special day, and I wanted to be here so I could tell the boys and girls a story.

Pastor: Very good, Peter. Go ahead. They are all ears, I am sure.

Peter: Boys and girls, there is an old story about a tiny acorn that had a great dream. He was tiny now, but one day he would be a giant oak tree spreading his limbs and casting an impressive shadow over everyone around him. Someday, perhaps someone would come, cut him down, and shape him into a giant sailing ship or a beautiful home. This tiny acorn had all these great dreams. A little sparrow who was a friend of his asked him if he really believed he would accomplish all that. "Yes," replied the little acorn, "God and I will."

Pastor: Peter, that story reminds me of how thirty years ago a small group of men and women here in our city dreamed of a great new church — this church. They knew that with God's help they could do it.

Peter: That doesn't mean that God was going to do all the work. Pastor, why don't we tell the boys and girls what went into the building of our church?

Pastor: That's a good idea, Peter. Why don't you start?

Peter: Well, first of all they had to have a Vision. They put their *dreams* into the new church because they had a vision of what it would mean to the community.

Pastor: They also had to have Faith. They had Faith that they could be used by God to bring their Dreams into reality.

Peter: Yes, and don't forget Prayer. They couldn't do it on their own, so they spent a good deal of time praying about it.

Pastor: Let's not forget that they had to be Willing To Work. They knew that Faith without Works is meaningless. So they had to be willing to work to make their dreams come true.

Peter: Of course, that meant Sacrificial Giving of Time, Talents, and Money. They were prepared to make sacrifices and to give generously to bring this new church into being.

Pastor: Let's not forget Lay Leadership. Any task takes good leadership, and they had that.

Peter: That good leadership included Pastoral Leadership. To build a church you have to have good pastoral leadership, and they had that, too.

Pastor: Even with all that they put into it they couldn't accomplish the task on their own. They received generous help from another church in town and from the Annual Conference.

Peter: Most important of all, Pastor, they relied on God's leadership and guidance through the Holy Spirit.

Pastor: You're absolutely right, Peter, and today we celebrate the birthday of our church. We enjoy the fruit of all they put into it, and we have to pledge ourselves to keep working to make our church even better for the future.

Peter: What do you suppose we would get, Pastor, if we put all those ingredients that went into the founding of our church into your fireless cooker?

Pastor: Well, let's try it and see. (*Place pieces of paper marked with the ingredients such as Faith, Prayer, etc., into magic pan which has been loaded with a birthday cake*) There, what do we have? A birthday cake! Let's all sing "Happy Birthday" to our church!

Fight The Good Fight

Pastor: Wow, what happened to you, Peter?

Peter: Well, I got into this fight with Big Bad Bill.

Pastor: Boy, that wasn't the right thing to do!

Peter: Oh, yes, it was! The Bible says we're to fight if we have to. It calls us soldiers. Why just the other day I read a verse telling us to fight the good fight of faith. And this fight wasn't just good; it was great!

Pastor: That's not what that verse was talking about. It's telling us to defend our faith in Jesus Christ.

Peter: That's just what I was doing. You see, my Sunday school teacher said we should witness. So today I was talking to some kids about Jesus, when Big Bad Bill came along.

Pastor: What happened then?

Peter: Well, when he heard what I was saying, he said all Christians are a bunch of sissies. So I said we are not sissies, and to prove it, I put a block of wood on my shoulder and told him to knock it off if he could.

Pastor: By the way you look, I'd say he knocked it off, all right.

Peter: Yeah, but I won! If you think I look bad, you should see Big Bad Bill. He's not so bad any more. He has two black eyes and a fat lip.

Pastor: Oh, boy, that's too bad!

Peter: No, it's not. I sat on Big Bad Bill until he gave in, and then I sat on him some more and asked him if he wanted to be a Christian, too!

Pastor: Oh, no! Peter, that's not how to witness.

Peter: Why not? I was fighting for Jesus, and I told Big Bad Bill about him.

Pastor: We can't witness by fighting. We witness in love and kindness. You can't force anyone to be a Christian. A person must believe in Jesus because he or she wants to.

Peter: But how can I make him want to be a Christian? I thought it was by showing how tough we can be.

Pastor: People come to Jesus because of love and kindness, not fighting.

Peter: But I can't just stand there and let Big Bad Bill make fun of me.

Pastor: Jesus did.

Peter: He did?

Pastor: Yes. He let people make fun of him, and he didn't say a word. But he wasn't a sissy. He took all their sins on himself so they could be saved.

Peter: I see what you mean. I bet Big Bad Bill doesn't really know anything about Jesus.

Pastor: He's watching you to see what Jesus is like.

Peter: Boy, I didn't act like Jesus at all. I'd better go tell Big Bad Bill how sorry I am. I hope he will forgive me and let me start over.

Pastor: Start over fighting again?

Peter: No, no. Start over with love.

Pastor: Now that's fighting the good fight.

Moms Are Like That

Pastor: Good morning, Peter. Why are you looking so sad?

Peter: Good morning, Pastor. Well, you know that new baseball mitt I wanted?

Pastor: Yes! Did you get it?

Peter: Well, I thought I had figured out a way to pay for it but I got more than I bargained for!

Pastor: Oh! What was your great scheme?

Peter: You know my mom sits down once a month to pay bills. So I wondered what would happen if I slipped my own bill in with all the others.

Pastor: And what did you bill your mom for?

Peter: Well, I figured if I charged her $1.50 for each of my chores it would cover it. So I wrote out a regular bill:

Peter's Bill To Mom	
Taking out the trash	$1.50
Carrying in groceries	1.50
Help with the dishes	1.50
Make my bed (Saturdays)	1.50
Practice the piano	1.50
Pick up my clothes	1.50
Total —	$9.00

Pastor: Well, how did it work?

Peter: You'll never guess what was under my breakfast plate this morning.

33

Pastor: You got the money?

Peter: Yep. I got the money — $9.00; but more importantly, I got something to think about. I also got a bill from Mom.

Pastor: You're kidding! Your mom gave you a bill? For how much?

Peter: It was marked zero — no charge. Here's what it said:

Mom's Bill To Peter

For three good hot meals a day	0
For taking care of Peter when he's sick	0
For taking care of Peter's puppy when Peter is tired	0
For washing and ironing Peter's clothes	0
For helping with homework	0
For a good home and lots of love	0
Total — Zero	

Pastor: Well, how do you feel now?

Peter: I feel somewhat ashamed of myself. Now I understand why the Bible says, "It is more blessed to give than to receive."

Pastor: Maybe that's why your mom always seems so happy. She gives so much and giving makes her happy ... just like the Bible says!

Peter: Yeah, I guess moms are like that. I love you, Mom!

Sin Protection

Peter: Get your sin protection here! "Sin Protectors" — only $5 each or two for $15. Don't be fooled by cheap imitations; get the original "Sin Protector" here! Get your sin ...

Pastor: Peter, what is that thing on your head?

Peter: Oh, hi, Pastor! This is a new invention of mine. I call it a "Sin Protector."

Pastor: It looks just like a lightning rod.

Peter: Shh! Not so loud — are you trying to put me out of business? It is a lightning rod — but if people don't know that, I can call it a "Sin Protector" and double the price!

Pastor: But how can a lightning rod protect you from sin?

Peter: Not from sin, Dummy — it protects you from the wrath of God!

Pastor: The wrath of God?

Peter: Yeah! You see, I figure that Christians are a pretty nervous lot, knowing that God's watching you all the time. I mean, one little slip up — one little sin — and it's BLAMO! Hello, lightning; good-bye, Christian. This little lightning rod should be just the thing to let you guys relax and have a little fun every so often.

Pastor: Oh, Peter, you've got it all wrong. God doesn't tell us not to sin just so he can punish us when we slip up. God loves us too much ever to do anything like that.

Peter: Then why doesn't he want you to have any fun?

Pastor: He does! But sometimes what we think is fun is really bad for us.

Peter: What do you mean?

Pastor: Well, when you were really small did you think it was fun to play with matches?

Peter: Sure — only my dad always hid them so I couldn't play with them. But one time I tricked him — I found the matches and started playing with them when he wasn't around.

Pastor: And what happened?

Peter: Well, I guess I kinda burned my fingers.

Pastor: Now do you understand why God doesn't want us to sin?

Peter: Oh, I get it! It's not that God doesn't want us to have fun; it's just that he cares for us and knows what's good for us even when we don't know ourselves!

Pastor: Exactly!

Peter: I guess you're right. But if God isn't waiting to shoot lightning bolts at any minute, how am I going to sell these "Sin Protectors"?

Pastor: Oh, I'm sure you'll think of something.

Peter: Hmmm. Get your donut holders here! "Donut Racks" — only $5 each or two for $15. Don't be fooled by cheap imitations....

Honoring Mothers

Peter: Good morning, Pastor. Are we honoring mothers today?

Pastor: Yes, Peter, this is their special day. Why do you ask?

Peter: Well, I have some advice to give mothers.

Pastor: What kind of advice do you have?

Peter: Mothers sometimes want to be alone. Right?

Pastor: Right!

Peter: All mother has to do is start doing the dishes. Know what my mother told me the other day?

Pastor: That's hard to say.

Peter: She told me to quit carrying frogs around in my pockets.

Pastor: That is a silly thing to carry around in your pockets, isn't it?

Peter: That may be true, but you should see what my mother carries around in her purse ... I don't really understand my mother.

Pastor: You don't? Why?

Peter: How come every time my mother gets tired, she makes *me* take a nap.

Pastor: Well, how about singing a song for the mothers?

Peter: Sure thing. How about, "You Ain't Nothin' But A Hound Dog"?

Pastor: I don't think mothers like that kind of song.

Peter: Then how about, "On Top Of Old Smokey"?

Pastor: This has to be a song just for mothers.

Peter: Okay, I'll sing the mothers' song. *M* is for the money that she gives me.

Pastor: No, no! *M* is for the million things she gives me.

Peter: That's what I said. *M* is for the money she gives me so I can buy a million things. What letter is after *M*?

Pastor: *O*.

Peter: Oh what?

Pastor: *M, O*.

Peter: Oh! You mean *O*. *O* means that you're over the hill.

Pastor: *O* means that she's growing older.

Peter: But my mom said when you hit thirty, you're over the hill.

Pastor: Next is the letter is *T*.

Peter: Okay. *T* is for the trillion times she spanked me.

Pastor: I agree.

Peter: You mean, I sang it right?

Pastor: Not really. *T* is for the tears she sheds for me.

Peter: But I'm the one who sheds the tears every time she spanks me. What letter comes after *T*?

Pastor: *H*.

Peter: God bless you!

Pastor: Peter, I didn't sneeze. I said, "*H*."

Peter: Ah, yes. *H* is for her hair — you never know what color it's going to be tomorrow.

Pastor: No, Peter. *H* is for her hair of pure gold.

Peter: Not my mother. It's more like dishwater blonde.

Pastor: Be nice.

Peter: Okay. Next is *E*. *E* is for her ever-rising temper.

Pastor: *E* is for her ever-loving service.

Peter: Yeah, but her temper is always rising around me.

Pastor: Do you ever make your mom mad at you?

Peter: Once in a while. But I'm really not a bad kid, you know.

Pastor: I know. The last letter is *R*.

Peter: *R* is for her rushing me. My mom rushes me here, there, and everywhere.

Pastor: *R* means right, and right she'll always be, because she means the world to me.

Peter: I love my mother.

Pastor: Well, that was really sweet of you to say, Peter.

Peter: Yeah, I had to say it. I just remembered, my mother is in the congregation.

Pastor: Oh, that's right! Your mother is going to be upset with you for being so silly. Peter, do you remember what the Bible says about mothers?

Peter: Does it say that they are to be seen and not heard?

Pastor: No, Peter, the Bible doesn't say that about anyone. Do you remember the Ten Commandments?

Pastor: Kind of.

Pastor: Do you remember the one that says to honor your mother and father?

Peter: Oh, yeah!

Pastor: Did you know that was the only commandment that had a promise added to it?

Peter: What kind of promise?

Pastor: Well, it was the very first commandment that God gave. So it must have been important. Don't you think so, Peter?

Peter: Oh, yeah!

Pastor: If you honor your mother and father, the promise is that things will go well with you and you will enjoy a long life on the earth.

Peter: I'm gonna listen to my mom. I really do love her. She's the sweetest, kindest, most wonderfullest mother in the world. I couldn't have made it without her, if you know what I mean.

Pastor: I think now would be a good time to tell these nice people good-bye.

Peter: Good-bye, and it's been fun being with you!

"Just Say No"

Pastor: What's that big button you're wearing for, Peter?

Peter: Haven't you heard? We are starting a "Just Say No" club here at the church.

Pastor: "Just Say No" — what kind of club is that?

Peter: Jesus taught us to say, "No," to the devil. Right?

Pastor: Right — every time the devil tempted him, Jesus said, "No."

Peter: Well, we kids want to learn to "Just Say No" to drugs and alcohol.

Pastor: That sounds really smart, because if you want to stay healthy and happy you have to remain drug-free.

Peter: I know! If I want to amount to something, I have to have a clear mind. Drugs can ruin your life.

Pastor: Some people say it is hard to say, "No," to your friends.

Peter: Maybe, but it is still harder to get straight once you're on drugs. By the way, you know some people also say you'll end up without any friends if you don't use drugs.

Pastor: With friends like that, you're better off without them. Let me tell you, Peter, I've said, "No," to drugs and alcohol all my life, and I still have lots of friends.

Peter: Well, that's what we want to teach kids in our new club. We're going to show them that they can have lots of fun without drugs and alcohol.

Pastor: How old do you have to be to join your club?

Peter: Boys and girls from kindergarten on up are welcome.

Pastor: And where can parents learn more about it?

Peter: This Wednesday, following the Fellowship Dinner, we are going to show the video with Punkie Brewster that tells all about it.

So, boys and girls, get your parents to bring you Wednesday night and you can join our "Just Say No" club!

"Just Say No" II

Pastor: Good morning, Peter! What's that shirt you're wearing?

Peter: Good morning to you, Pastor. This is my "Just Say No" shirt. I got this three years ago when I joined the "Just Say No" club here at church. Now they have these clubs in schools, and we have just finished celebrating "Just Say No" Week.

Pastor: That's wonderful, Peter. I'm so happy that a great many boys and girls are learning the important lesson of saying, "No," to drugs and alcohol.

Peter: By the way, Pastor, I have a question for you. Do you know who formed the first "Just Say No" Club?

Pastor: Well, I was going to say Adam; but when Eve tempted him with the apple, he forgot to say, "No." I give up.

Peter: Shadrak, Meshak, and Abednego — when Nebuchadnezzar decreed that they must give up their religion and worship him they just said, "No."

Pastor: Did that save them?

Peter: Oh, no. The king threw them into the fiery furnace of temptation, but God saved them. That's the way it is with us. We boys and girls are learning that we can face the temptations of drugs, alcohol, and smoking, but God will give us the strength to resist if we "Just Say No"!

Pastor: Very good. That's an important lesson for all of us to learn.

Peter: You bet it is. It would be great if the grown-ups would get wise, too, and learn to say, "No," to drugs, alcohol, and smoking.

They would be better off, and they would be setting a good example for their children and grandchildren.

Pastor: I notice you have a baseball cap on this morning, Peter.

Peter: That's right, Pastor, and it's not because I play baseball. I want people to know that in this game of life I play on a team called St. John's Children of God. We try hard to win other people to God's side. It is because of the training I get here in church and Sunday school that I get the help I need to resist temptation and "Just Say No." You're on the team, Pastor. Why don't you get a hat?

Pastor: As a matter of fact I have one, Peter; and today is the last day that people in the congregation can order them, so they had better hurry. Time to say good-bye now.

Peter: "Good-bye now." Have a good week, boys and girls, and remember to "Just Say No" to all those bad things like drugs, alcohol, and smoking!

Camp Presentation

Pastor: Good morning, Peter. What have you been up to?

Peter: Well, in school I'm up to the six times table, and last night I was up to nine o'clock. What about you?

Pastor: Peter, you know what I mean. Just before church I saw you making a list.

Peter: Oh, I'm getting ready for camp. It's less than two months away.

Pastor: How can you get ready this early? You can't pack your clothes yet! You'll need them.

Peter: Oh, I'm just making a list.

Pastor: Say, that's a good idea. Then you won't forget to pack the things you need. Do you have down your Bible, a notebook, a flashlight, and bug spray?

Peter: Well, no, ah ... it's not that kind of list.

Pastor: Well, what kind is it? Tell me.

Peter: Maybe you could help me add to it. You've been to camp before, haven't you?

Pastor: Oh, sure. I had a great time. We learned about Jesus, played games, went swimming, did crafts, sang songs, and I made some neat new Christian friends ... Wow, I could go on and on. But back to your list — let me hear it.

Peter: What kind of camp are you talking about? That's not what I heard about camp.

Pastor: I went to a Methodist Camp, and it was great. But quit stalling, I want to hear your list.

Peter: No, I don't think I want to read it after all.

Pastor: Let me help you. (*Reaches over and takes list*)
1. Find a frog or snake.
2. Practice whistling.
3. Bring plenty of shaving cream.
4. Learn to short-sheet a bed.

Peter: Well, I heard people go to camp to play tricks on each other.

Pastor: I understand the frog, but why whistling?

Peter: Don't they whistle at the pretty girls? (*Whistles*)

Pastor: And what about shaving cream? You don't shave.

Peter: You don't know anything!

Pastor: I think you've got the wrong idea about camp, Peter. You go to camp to learn more about Jesus, and have fun with Christian friends.

Peter: Boy, did I get told wrong. Guess I'd better rip up the list I made.

Pastor: Oh, don't be hasty ... camp is also a time for fun, and jokes can add to the fun as long as they don't hurt anyone. But be sure to *register*!

Rise And Shine

Pastor: Hello, everyone. Today I've asked Peter to lead us in a prayer. Are you ready, Peter?

Peter: I sure am. (*Rings a bell*) Okay, Lord! Rise and shine!

Pastor: Wait a minute. What's the bell for?

Peter: I was just making sure God was awake, so he could hear us when we pray.

Pastor: What?

Peter: Well, you never know. He might be taking a nap or something. So I thought I'd better make sure he was awake before we pray.

Pastor: Peter, you don't have to worry about that. You don't have to wake God up.

Peter: I don't?

Pastor: No. You see, Psalm 121 says that God never slumbers or sleeps. He's always there when we want to talk to him.

Peter: Doesn't God ever get tired?

Pastor: No. God is so strong and so powerful that he never gets tired.

Peter: Wow!

Pastor: Are you ready to lead us in prayer now?

Peter: Yep. (*Rings bell again*)

Pastor: Hold it, I just told you, you don't have to wake God up.

Peter: I know. I just want to get his attention. There may be lots of people praying now. I want to be sure that he pays attention to us, so he'll know what we're praying for.

Pastor: Peter, you don't have to worry about that, either.

Peter: I don't?

Pastor: No. God always hears us when we pray. Even if everyone else in the whole world were praying at the same time, God would hear what we say.

Peter: How can he do that?

Pastor: Because God is everywhere, and he knows everything. Whenever and wherever we pray, he'll be there, and he'll hear us.

Peter: Wow! Is that true? That means God's really wonderful, doesn't it? He's always awake, and always listening, and always ready to help us. Are you ready to pray now, everybody? Let's bow our heads.

Dear God, thank you for listening to us. Help us to love everyone as much as you love us. Help us always to remember to be kind, and caring, and forgiving. Help us to do all the things you tell us to do in the Bible. Help us to love you and Jesus even more every day. Amen.

The Good Shepherd And The Flock

Pastor: Good morning, Peter. It's good to have you with us this morning.

Peter: Good morning, Pastor. It's good to be here this morning; especially since we have John Riley as our special guest.

Pastor: Oh, you like John Riley, do you?

Peter: I sure do. He's a country boy, like I am. And I am particularly happy because he has been talking about one of my favorite Bible persons.

Pastor: Oh? Who's that?

Peter: David. You know he wrote a lot of our Psalms?

Pastor: Yes, I knew that.

Peter: Did you also know that David was a shepherd?

Pastor: Yes, I think I heard that.

Peter: Well, that's why I am especially glad John is talking about him. (You don't mind if I call you John, do you?) You see David knew all about shepherds and how they take care of their sheep — leading them into green pastures and beside still waters where they could drink, and protecting them from wild animals. And David taught us that the Lord is our Shepherd.

Pastor: That's right, Peter; and Psalm 23 is one of my favorites. It tells us that the Lord is our Shepherd, we shall not want.

Peter: Well, did you know that Jesus is the Good Shepherd? He taught us that the Good Shepherd cares for his sheep, knows them by name, and if any go astray, he isn't happy until he goes after them and finds them and brings them safely back to the flock.

Pastor: Yes, I knew that. Does all this have anything to do with that shirt you are wearing, Peter?

Peter: It sure does. You see, Jesus has so many sheep that in order to take care of them, he gathers them together in *Flocks*, we call the Church. He has assistant shepherds — like you — that help him take care of his sheep. I belong to his Flock here at our church, and when I go to Sunday school events, or sports, or informal church gatherings, I want everyone to know which Flock I belong to. And besides it makes it easier for you shepherds to keep an eye on me ... ha, ha.

Pastor: Say, that's a neat idea. Can anybody here in our church get one of those shirts?

Peter: You bet. The Sunday school is selling them and they will be glad to take your order.

Pastor: Do you think they would even have one to fit me?

Peter: Yes, even you. So hurry, folks. We are all part of our church's *Flock*, and we follow Jesus Christ, the Good Shepherd. Let's flock together as we wear our shirts.

Our Silent Partner

Pastor: Good morning, Peter. It's good to have you with us again.

Peter: It's good to be here, Pastor; besides I need the rest.

Pastor: Oh, have you been working hard this morning?

Peter: You bet. Can't you see I've been working in my garden?

Pastor: Oh, I didn't know you had a garden. Where is it?

Peter: Well, I found this empty lot that wasn't being used for anything but a dump. The owner said I could use it for a garden.

Pastor: Good for you. Was it much work getting it ready?

Peter: I'll say. First I had to clean up all the mess. There were cans, and bottles, and styrofoam cups, and newspapers. I gathered all these up and took what I could to the recycling bins here at church. Then I had to clear the stones, dig and rake, and finally plant my seeds. Some of them have already started to grow.

Pastor: Well, Peter, I guess you do deserve a rest.

Peter: You know, Pastor, a man walked by my garden the other day while I was working, and he said to me: "Peter, that certainly is a beautiful garden that you and God have there."

Pastor: That was nice of him.

Peter: You know what I said to him? I said: "Yes, but you should have seen it when God had it alone."

Pastor: It may sound funny, Peter, but you know it is true that you and God are partners in this garden.

Peter: Oh, I know that. God gives the sun and the rain — and the seeds and the miracle of growth.

Pastor: I'm glad you realize that, Peter. God doesn't make gardens grow alone, and neither do people. But when God and people work together, then the miracle of growth can take place in our gardens.

Peter: You know what else, Pastor?

Pastor: What?

Peter: Today is Earth Day, and all of us need to remember that it isn't only when we are working the garden that we are partners with God. It's all the time.

Pastor: That's right, Peter. The Bible teaches us that the Earth is the Lord's, and all that is in it. He put us here to take care of it, and God doesn't like it when we dirty the air, pollute the water, and rob the land of its riches.

Peter: Boys and girls, I hope you will always remember that you and God are partners, and he needs you to take care of this earth. So don't waste water. Learn to recycle your cans, bottles, and newspapers. Don't be a litter-bug.

Have a good week. Now let us pray together: Lord, we thank you for the sun, the rain, and the good earth. Help us to take good care of the wonderful world you have given us. Amen.

Keeping In Touch

(Puppet should pause between lines)

Peter: Hello, operator? I'd like to make a long distance call.

To which city? Heaven, please. I'd like to talk with God.

You say that's not a long-distance call? And I can call direct? Oh, but I've already been put through anyway? Thanks.

(Clears throat and says shyly) Hello. You may not remember me, Lord, but my name is Peter and ...

What's that? Oh, you know me well. Well, I was just wondering if it would be all right to talk with you for a while?

Really? I can talk to you any time and from any place? Imagine that. Why that's very nice of you, Sir. But then I've heard that's the way you are.

What? Oh, you're welcome. I didn't realize you like to hear nice things, too. But I guess everyone does, huh? Well, I was just wondering if you'd help me get a few things straightened out.

What? You thought I'd never ask? Well, I'm asking because I guess I've kind of made a mess out of things by myself.

Oh, you've noticed? Well, I heard that you make all things new and I think I could use a new start.

(Eagerly) What? You can help? Wow, that's great!

I'm supposed to do what?

Read the Bible. Uh-huh. And pray. Okay. Share my faith with others. Uh-huh. And follow your example. Gotcha. Whew! That's a lot.

There's more?

Use some of that talent you gave me? Okay. And you say you like to hear me sing? Uh-huh. And it wouldn't hurt to smile more? Oh, uh, right. I'll try to do better, Sir.

What? You'll be there to help? Why, thank you. That will make it easier.

You have a way of making things easier, I'll try to remember that. Well, it has been nice talking to you, Sir.

Oh, you're glad I called? I am, too. I'm feeling better already.

What? Keep in touch? Oh, yeah. I will. I really will. Good-bye, Sir.

(*Puts phone down and looks upward*) And thanks again for being there!

Know When To Duck

Pastor: Good morning, Peter. Did you like your Sunday school lesson today?

Peter: I sure did. It's one of my favorite stories.

Pastor: What was it about?

Peter: A little boy about my size, named David. With a little slingshot and one stone he killed great big giant Goliath.

Pastor: All by himself?

Peter: No! God did it through David.

Pastor: Well, Peter, that is an exciting story.

Peter: It sure is, Pastor. Why our Sunday school teacher told the story so well I could almost see the stone flying through the air and landing right in Goliath's forehead. Then I could see him fall like a great big tree to the ground. I could almost feel the earth shaking as he hits.

Pastor: That's fine, Peter, but what does the story tell us?

Peter: Tell us?

Pastor: Yes, what should we remember from this story?

Peter: Ummm, I'm not sure. Is the point of the story that we need to know when to duck? Yeah, that's it. If Goliath had ducked, he wouldn't have been killed.

Pastor: No, Peter, that's not what the story teaches.

Peter: Good, 'cause I don't think I could always learn the right time to duck. What does it teach us, Pastor?

Pastor: That we need to trust and obey God's word.

Peter: Obey?

Pastor: Yes, we need to listen carefully to what God is saying to us in the Bible. And then, trusting him, we need to be obedient.

Peter: I understand! If David hadn't listened and obeyed God, then God wouldn't have used him to kill Goliath. And God's people would still be fighting Goliath.

Pastor: Well, not still fighting Goliath, but they would have had it a lot harder.

Peter: Thanks, Pastor. Boy, what a stupid answer — it teaches us to duck. Well, come to think of it, that's a very important thing to learn, too!

A Direct Line To Jesus

Pastor: Peter, I saw you looking in the phone book. What are you doing, anyway? Trying to find your home phone number?

Peter: No, Pastor. I know my number. I know the emergency number of my doctor. I know the 911 number for police and fire departments. I know the church office number; but I don't ... I don't know ...

Pastor: You don't know what, Peter?

Peter: I want to call Jesus! But I don't know his number.

Pastor: Well, have you looked in the book?

Peter: I sure have. I've looked under *J* for Jesus, *H* for heaven, *L* for Lord — but so far nothing.

Pastor: Peter, that phone book will help you find useful numbers, but to call Jesus, look in your Bible.

Peter: I think you're confused, Pastor. The Bible has verses in it, not phone numbers.

Pastor: Listen to this from Psalm 4 verse 3: "The Lord hears when I call to him." And Psalm 145 verse 18 says: "The Lord is near to all who call upon him ... in truth."

Peter: Hey, I can do that without a telephone!

Pastor: Sure. When you call through your prayers, Jesus will always be listening; no matter what time of day or night it may be.

Peter: Wow! I can talk to Jesus! Say, where is that phone?

Pastor: Peter, I just told you that you don't need a phone to do that.

Peter: Oh, I know. I'm calling my mom to tell her it's time to pick me up. I'll be lucky if the line isn't busy. My sister is always yacking with her friends. Boy, I'm sure glad that Jesus' number is always working, and is never busy. Having a direct line to him is great!

Pastor: Yes, and you can't be disconnected either.

Peter: And best of all, there's no long distance charge!

Pastor: Remember, boys and girls, any time you want to talk with Jesus, all you have to do is *pray*.

The Bloofer Box

Pastor: Good morning, Peter. I'm glad you're here.

Peter: You know, I really didn't want to be here. I could have gone to the park with my friend.

Pastor: Why didn't you?

Peter: Oh, I didn't want to get up so early.

Pastor: Well, you can have a good time being with all these boys and girls in children's church.

Peter: Yeah, I guess. But then pretty soon I'll have to go home and set the table.

Pastor: Isn't that a blessing? Just think, you've got enough food to put on the table.

Peter: Oh, I suppose. But sometimes it's not very much fun to eat. My little sister cries and argues and throws her food around. And then we have to take a bath and go to bed.

Pastor: Hey, I think I'm beginning to understand what a bloofer is. (*To Congregation*) I'll say something, and I'll bet he bloofs. (*To Peter*) Let's get some ice cream after church.

Peter: It's too cold.

Pastor: Let's get a Big Mac.

Peter: It's too far away.

Pastor: Want to play a game?

Peter: Uh, uh. I'll lose.

Pastor: Isn't it wonderful to have eyes we can see with?

Peter: They're tired. I didn't get enough sleep last night.

Pastor: Boys and girls, have you figured out what a bloofer is? It's someone who complains all the time. Is a bloofer fun to be with? What can a bloofer do instead of bloofing? Do you think he could be thankful instead? What do you think, Bloofer Peter? Do you think if we called you Thankful Peter, that you would quit bloofing?

Peter: I'd like to try, 'cause it sure does get lonely and depressing when I bloof. Thank you for wanting to help me and be my friend, but it probably won't work.

Pastor: Hold it, that's a bloofer. I've got a bloofer box that might help you. (*Brings out a box*) Every time you or I bloof, we've got to put a penny in the box.

Peter: Oh, no, I'll be poor in no time.

Pastor: That's a bloof. Put in a penny.

Peter: (*Puts in a penny*) Now I only have nine cents left and I needed to get a pencil for ten cents.

Pastor: Put in another penny.

Peter: Oh, come on, this is ridiculous. (*Drops in a penny*)

Pastor: Make it two.

Peter: (*Drops in another penny*) But why can't I complain and get it out of my system?

Pastor: Because it says in the Bible, "Do all things without grumbling or complaining."

Peter: So?

Pastor: So, that's God's command. And whenever we obey him, we're happier.

Peter: Okay, I'll do it. I wonder if I can go through a whole day without putting in one bloofer penny? Do you think any of these kids can do that?

Pastor: Nah, kids always bloof.

Peter: Hey, that's a bloof. Pay up!

Pastor: Uh-oh. I've got to go and get some more pennies. Come on, let's go.

Respect For Older People

Peter: Why do I have to say, "Ma'am"? Why should I respect older people? Mom is always saying, "Remember to say, 'Please' and, 'Thank you,' and always say, 'Yes, sir,' or, 'No, sir.' (*Mocks his mother*) 'Don't run! You will run into someone.' " Well, who cares if I'm polite? I don't like being polite.

Pastor: What's going on, Peter?

Peter: Oh, I just got a spanking for not respecting my grandmother!

Pastor: Oh, Peter! (*In dismay*) What did you do?

Peter: I didn't say, "Yes, Ma'am," and forgot to say, "No, thank you" ... and on top of all that, I ran her over in church this morning.

Pastor: Peter, you didn't really run over her, did you?

Peter: No, I just sort of ... uh ... knocked her down.

Pastor: Well, good grief! Didn't you listen in Sunday school this morning?

Peter: Sure! I sang, and played with playdough, and I colored, and even said the memory verse!

Pastor: No, I mean, didn't you listen to the story?

Peter: You mean there was a story?

Pastor: Yes, there was a story!

Peter: Hmpf ... Well, I didn't hear one!

Pastor: I can tell, or you wouldn't have gotten into trouble. It told how we should respect our elders.

Peter: Oh, you mean the preachers of the church.

Pastor: It means all older people, not just the preachers past fifty. Don't you know the golden rule? "Do unto others as you would have them do unto you."

Peter: You mean, if I respect older people, they will respect me, too?

Pastor: Sure they will.

Peter: Wow! I'll try it. Maybe next time I won't get into trouble, as long as I remember the golden rule.

Pastor: Just remember to treat everyone the way you want to be treated. Would you want someone to run over you the way you ran over your poor grandmother?

Peter: No, I guess not. (*Pauses*) How about if we run over to my house for cookies?

Pastor: After all that, Peter, you still want to run?

Peter: Oh, yeah ... how about if we walk over to my house?

Pastor: That's better! I'd love some cookies!

Don't Wait Until The Season Is Over

Pastor: Wasn't that a great football game at the high school yesterday, Peter? (*No response*) I said wasn't that a great football game yesterday?

Peter: Oh, Pastor, I'm sorry. I had my mind on something else.

Pastor: So I see. Want to talk about it?

Peter: I was just thinking about what you said in your sermon last week.

Pastor: I said a lot of things in my sermon. I mean a lot of things! What part are you talking about?

Peter: The part about how important it is to accept Jesus into your heart while you're still young.

Pastor: That's true.

Peter: What's the difference as long as you do it before you die?

Pastor: Well, there are different reasons. For one, we don't know how long we will live and we might wait too long. But here's another one. Let me see ... how can I explain this? Peter, think about that football game we saw Saturday.

Peter: Okay. Now what?

Pastor: Let's compare it to your lifetime.

Peter: My lifetime? If I got tackled that many times in a day, my lifetime wouldn't be very long ... or very pleasant!

Pastor: Oh, Peter ... let me explain. Suppose you wanted to be on the team and you could join anytime you wanted. If you started in the training camp, you could prepare for the season, and if you were really good at something, say punting, or field goals ...

Peter: How about quarterback?

Pastor: Okay, quarterback. Anyway, you could spend time developing these areas, so you could do your best.

Peter: I can see me now ... Big Peter, the all-star! Rah! Rah! Rah!

Pastor: Simmer down, Big Peter, that's not the end of the story. What if you joined in the middle of the season? You would be limited as to what you could do.

Peter: Hmmm ...

Pastor: And finally, what if you became a member of the team after the season was over?

Peter: Well, that would mean I hadn't done anything but join the team.

Pastor: Exactly!

Peter: Exactly what, Pastor?

Pastor: When we accept Jesus early in life, we are starting out in training camp. We can study and prepare ourselves for whatever God wants us to do, like be a Sunday school teacher or a minister or a missionary. But the later you wait, the more opportunities you will miss in life.

Peter: Well, what do you mean about joining when the season is over?

Pastor: That would be someone who accepts Jesus just before they die. They will go to heaven, but that's all. Their life has already been spent.

Peter: I see! That's what you meant last Sunday when you said in your sermon "not just a soul saved, but a soul and a life."

Pastor: That's right, Peter.

Peter: Pastor, can I join Jesus' team today?

Pastor: You sure can, Peter. Let's pray about it right now.

Lord, we thank you for the opportunity you give us to be a part of your team. Help us to open our hearts to Jesus, so we may welcome him into our lives, and then help us to follow his commands, so we can be helpful members of your team. Amen.

The Sunday School Offering

Pastor: Peter, Sunday school has started. How come you're not in class?

Peter: I'm not going to class today.

Pastor: Not going to class! Look, Peter, everyone's going to class, including your mother. She wouldn't be too happy if she knew you were skipping Sunday school.

Peter: Well, she doesn't know, Pastor, and she won't know as long as a certain person keeps quiet about it.

Pastor: I'm not a tattletale! I just don't understand why you won't go to class. You like Sunday school, and go every week.

Peter: I know, Pastor, and I wanted to go today, but I just can't.

Pastor: Why can't you go?

(*Peter mumbles quietly*)

Pastor: What did you say?

Peter: Because I don't have any money! (*Pauses*) My father forgot to give me my quarter this morning, so I can't pay to get in. Now you know!

Pastor: Peter, you don't have to pay to get into Sunday school.

Peter: Oh, yes, we do. Every week when I get to class, I put a quarter in the basket.

Pastor: The money we put in the basket is our gift to Jesus. It's used to help other people, and to teach them about God. Sunday school is free, and you can go even when you don't have a gift to bring.

Peter: Free! Sunday school is free! Oh, wow! That's great! I'm going to class. (*Pauses*) Say, Pastor, just think — now that I know I don't have to pay to get in, I can save all my quarters and get a new game!

Pastor: You've got it all wrong, Peter! You've misunderstood what I said!

Peter: No, I didn't, Pastor. I understood the whole thing. I know when we have a gift, we need to share it by putting it in the offering. I just wanted to tease you.

Pastor: Boys and girls, let us have a prayer together: Father in heaven, we thank you for our Sunday school, which is free to all of us, and for the opportunities we have to share with others the good news of your wonderful love by the gifts we bring as we present our offerings to you. Amen.

Where's The Berries?

Pastor: Peter, your mom tells me you don't want to go to Sunday school any more.

Peter: That's right!

Pastor: Why, Peter?

Peter: Well ... it's so boring. I've heard all those stories.

Pastor: I'm sure you have. But the Bible is more than just stories. It helps us know how we should act and live for Jesus.

Peter: Aw, Pastor, I know all those things. I've been in Sunday school all my life, and I've even read the Bible through twice.

Pastor: Good! But you can still learn new things from it. No one has learned all that the Bible has to teach. I know I haven't.

Peter: You haven't? But you ... I mean, I thought ministers knew everything about the Bible.

Pastor: Oh, I wouldn't say that! There are many things in the Bible that I haven't learned yet.

Peter: Really?

Pastor: Peter, remember when we went picking blueberries the other day. It didn't look like there would be even enough berries to put on your cereal.

Peter: Yeah, not even enough for half a scoop of ice cream and berries.

Pastor: But then we started to look under the leaves, and the more we looked, the more berries we found. And I'll bet if we went back to where we've already picked, we could still find more!

Peter: Well, what does that have to do with me and Sunday school?

Pastor: Peter, looking for berries is like looking at the Bible. The more we study the Bible, the more we can learn. And then if we study the same part later, we may learn something new.

Peter: You mean I could learn something new from ... David and Goliath?

Pastor: Why don't you try?

Peter: Hmmm. Maybe I should keep going to Sunday school. I do want to learn more.

Pastor: Ask God to help you listen and learn. You've got to look through the leaves of your Bible yourself, too, Peter, to find the "berry" good things there!

Peter: Right! And after church, Pastor, what do you say we go to my house and have a piece of pie and a big scoop of ice cream?

Free Air

(Pastor does some deep breathing exercises)

Peter: Pastor, what in the world are you doing?

Pastor: I'm enjoying one of God's gifts. *(Breathes deeply again)* So are you.

Peter: Huh? God hasn't given me any gifts.

Pastor: Sure he has. This particular gift is all around us.

Peter: *(Looks all around)* I don't see anything. Not a single thing.

Pastor: *(Takes another deep breath)* It's the air we're breathing, Peter. It's a wonderful gift from God.

Peter: I don't want any gifts from God, and I'm not going to take any either! I'll just hold my breath. *(Takes a deep breath and snaps his mouth shut — after a while suddenly expels his breath and pants)*

Pastor: Change your mind?

Peter: I don't want any gifts from God. I know, I'll buy my own air!

Pastor: And just how are you going to do that?

Peter: I'll put extra money in the collection plate at church. That's what I'll do, buy my air!

Pastor: Peter, you can't pay for a gift that someone has already given you for free. Did you know that there is another gift that people try to buy from God?

Peter: No, what is it?

Pastor: Salvation.

Peter: Salvation?

Pastor: Yes, God gave us his Son, Jesus Christ. Jesus gave his life to pay for our sins. Some people try to pay for their sins by doing good works. The gift has already been given, though, so they can't pay.

Peter: What? You mean I've been doing all of those good deeds for nothing?

Pastor: Not for nothing, Peter. We do good deeds because we love God, not to buy something from him.

Peter: Oh!

Pastor: Actually, accepting the air you breathe and accepting Jesus are very much alike.

Peter: In what way?

Pastor: Well, you have to accept God's gift of air to live. Otherwise your body would die.

Peter: Oh, I get it. I have to accept God's gift of Jesus if I want to live eternally with him.

Pastor: That's right.

Peter: Thanks for setting me straight, Pastor. I do want to live eternally with God. It's good to know that I can accept his gift!

Lox vs. Pork Chops

Pastor: Hello, Peter. What are you up to?

Peter: Oh, hi, Pastor. I'm just going grocery shopping.

Pastor: Doesn't your mom usually do the shopping? What's the big occasion?

Peter: I'm having my friend, Abe Levitt, over for dinner. Mom said I could pick out what I want to eat!

Pastor: Well, it sounds like fun! My wife and I had Abe's parents over for dinner the other night.

Peter: Oh, yeah? What did you have to eat?

Pastor: Well, you know Mr. Levitt and his family are very devout Jews, so in their honor, my wife cooked a kosher meal.

Peter: A what meal?

Pastor: Kosher. You see, in the Jewish faith some foods are considered unclean or nonkosher.

Peter: Oh, yeah. I remember something in the Bible about that. But didn't we learn in church that all foods are considered clean by God?

Pastor: To the Christian, all foods are considered clean and good to eat. But in the Jewish religion, the Old Testament law is still followed, which says that certain foods are not to be eaten, while other foods are all right.

Peter: Yeah, but if the New Testament says that all foods are okay, why do we still have to follow the Old Testament?

Pastor: You and your family should follow what you believe when you're eating by yourselves, but when you have a guest, you need to respect their beliefs. The Bible has something to say on this subject. It says: "If your brother is distressed because of what you eat, you are no longer acting in love. Do not by your eating destroy your brother for whom Christ died." Do you understand, Peter?

Peter: Yeah, I think I'm beginning to. By fixing kosher food, I can show Abe that I care about him and I love him, even though we have different beliefs.

Pastor: Yes, and in return, as your friendship grows, Abe will respect your beliefs, too.

Peter: Uh. Pastor, are pork chops kosher?

Pastor: No, Peter. I'm afraid not. May I make a few suggestions?

Peter: Thanks, Pastor. I think I need a new shopping list now!

God's Gifts

Pastor: Hi, Peter. You look happy today.

Peter: Pastor, it's great to be seven years old.

Pastor: I'll bet it is, Peter, but do you know what? It's great to be any age.

Peter: But it's better to be seven.

Pastor: Maybe you think so, but each age has something good about it. I think it is nice to be my age.

Peter: But you don't like to play baseball.

Pastor: That's right, Peter, but I did when I was your age.

Peter: You did?

Pastor: Sure, but God has a way of maturing our minds with our bodies, so now I don't want to play ball. There are many other things I like to do. Many things I enjoy now that you can, too.

Peter: What's that?

Pastor: Well, sometimes I sit on the front porch, close my eyes and feel the warmth of the sun. It makes me feel close to God because the warmth of the sun is one of God's gifts to us. It gives me time to thank him for his gifts.

Peter: I like to play ball in the sun!

Pastor: Well, Peter, at one time I was too busy to stop and enjoy some of the things God has given us. I was too busy to take time to thank him for the wonderful things he has given us.

Peter: I always like to play ball.

Pastor: Yes, Peter, but we must stop and thank God for your ability to play ball. You see, I thank God for you.

Peter: For me?

Pastor: Peter, even though I don't want to play ball, I enjoy watching you play. You see, Peter, I love you.

Peter: And I love you, Pastor.

Pastor: Love is a gift from God, too, Peter.

Peter: I know, but I want to go play ball now ... Pastor, before I go ... will you pray with me and let's thank God for his gifts to us?

Pastor: Of course, Peter.

Boys and girls, let us pray together: Oh, Lord, our God, we thank you for your many gifts to us, and especially for the gift of love and good friends. Yes, and we thank you for the times we have or have had in days gone by to play ball. Amen.

Memory Work

Pastor: (*To the congregation*) Do you hear something? It sounds like somebody is singing. (*Pauses with his hand to his ear*) There it is again!

Peter: (*Singing to the tune of "How Great Thou Art"*) How great I am, how great I am. Then sings my soul, I am so wonderful ...

Pastor: Peter, what are you doing, anyway?

Peter: I was just singing.

Pastor: Well, you had the words all wrong. That's supposed to be a song of praise to God. The words should be, "How Great Thou Art."

Peter: I know I shouldn't change the words like that. I was just really excited.

Pastor: Oh, really? About what?

Peter: Our Sunday school teacher has been wanting us to memorize Bible verses! I didn't want to. I have to memorize spelling words at school, and I don't like that. But I decided to try it the other day.

Pastor: Oh? And how did it go?

Peter: Great! I found out that I'm good at it. I'm better than good. I'm fantastic! I'll bet I'm the best memorizer in the whole world.

Pastor: Well, Peter, you see ...

Peter: (*Interrupts*) Did you know that John 3:16 says: "For God so loved the world ..."

Pastor: (*Interrupts*) Hold it! ... Have you memorized Colossians 3:23 yet?

Peter: No. What does it say?

Pastor: It says: "And whatsoever you do, do it heartily as to the Lord, and not unto men." That means we should do everything for the Lord, and not to impress others. Do you see the connection?

Peter: Yes. I guess I'd better not memorize verses anymore.

Pastor: I wouldn't say that. Memorizing scripture is good for us, but we need to do it so that we can bring more glory to God.

Peter: I see now. I'd better work on that verse you just quoted. What was it again?

Pastor: Colossians 3:23. Let's go look it up together.

Singing Hymns For Him

(Peter hums "Home On The Range")

Pastor: Peter, what's that awful noise I hear?

Peter: Huh? What?

Pastor: Don't tell me that with those good ears of yours, you didn't hear those terrible sounds?

Peter: Er, uh, what did it sound like?

Pastor: Well, being a singer myself, it sounded like someone was trying to vocalize.

Peter: Vocalize?

Pastor: Yeah. You know, practice their singing.

Peter: Oh, ooh. That was meee!

Pastor: Really, Peter? What were you practicing for?

Peter: For choir, of course! I hear the choir is looking for new members, so I'm practicing to audition. Want to hear me sing a solo?

Pastor: I don't really think so, Peter. You see, we don't have auditions for the choir. Anyone can join. Besides, you have never sung before an audience. It would be rather embarrassing.

Peter: For whom? Me or you?

Pastor: Aw, now, Peter. Don't put it that way.

Peter: Let's ask the folks if they want to hear me sing. Everyone who wants to hear me sing, raise your hand. (*Raises his own hand and waits for the congregation to respond*)

Pastor: Okay, Peter. They do want to hear you sing. Go ahead.

Peter: (*Makes a great show of cleaning his throat. Sings to the tune of "Home On The Range"*)
Oh, give me a choir.
Where the ranks won't expire,
And the singers are happy all day.
Where always is heard
A melodious word,
And with spirit their church they inspire.

(*Chorus*)
Sing, sing in the choir,
Where with songs others' hearts we inspire.
To sing at our best,
But with no joining test,
Come, sing with us in our church choir.

Pastor: Hey, Peter, that's a great song! Everyone give Peter a big hand.

Peter: (*Takes a bow*) Thank you. Thank you, very much.

Pastor: Thank you, Peter. You helped me give a very important message. We are looking for new choir members, and anyone is welcome to join.

Who Said That?

Peter: (*Talking on the telephone*) Hello, Norman? This is Peter. Are you doing anything right now? Well, dry yourself off and pack up your stuff, and get out of your house before three o'clock ... That's right, three o'clock ... Why? Because the ground is going to open up and swallow your street. Okay ... See you.

Pastor: Peter, what are you doing?

Peter: Hi. I just saved Norman's life.

Pastor: I heard you telling him to get out of his house before the street gets swallowed up, but where did you get such an idea?

Peter: I heard it from Brother Hoodat down on the street corner. He says that God told him unless someone gives him a brand new Cadillac by three o'clock, the ground is going to open up and swallow Elm Street.

Pastor: What?

Peter: Right. And I know that I can't give Brother Hoodat a brand new Cadillac, so I thought I'd better call my friend Norman and warn him, 'cause he lives on Elm Street, right across from my mom and dad. (*Pauses*) My mom and dad! Quick, Pastor, give me the phone!

Pastor: Peter, you don't need the phone.

Peter: Pastor, this is no time for a lecture.

Pastor: You don't need the phone, because you don't need to call your parents. The ground isn't going to open up at three o'clock just because this Brother Whatshisname says so.

Peter: But, Pastor, it isn't just Brother Hoodat who says so. He says that he's only repeating what God told him to.

Pastor: Peter, all he is trying to do is get a new car for free. God didn't tell him that Elm Street would get swallowed up.

Peter: He didn't?

Pastor: No. If God wants Brother Whoozits to have a Cadillac, he'll provide a way for him to get one. But does threatening to wreck a street sound like how God would do it?

Peter: Well, no ... not really. But Brother Hoodat read lots of verses from the Bible where God made storms happen and rocks fall from the sky and fire burn up stuff. He says that God can still do that.

Pastor: Of course, God can do anything he wants. But this Brother Whazzat isn't giving the reasons that God made those things happen, is he?

Peter: You know what? He isn't. He just says that God gets in a bad mood sometimes if people don't do what he wants, and that what he wants now is a brand new Cadillac for Brother Hoodat.

Pastor: Peter, God has spoken to everyone through his Word — the Bible. If someone comes along saying he has a message from God, but that message doesn't fit with what the Bible says, it's probably not worth listening to.

Peter: Thanks, Pastor. You've kept me from worrying all day about my family and Norman. Norman! Oh, Pastor, you've got to help me!

Pastor: What is it now?

Peter: We've got to help Norman get all his stuff back in his house! He's started moving already!

Pastor: But, Peter, he can't have gotten too far yet. Why don't you just call him? (*Hands the phone to Peter*)

"This Little Light Of Mine"

Peter: (*Holding flashlight, shines it all around and sings, slightly off key*)
This little light of mine
I'm gonna let it shine
This little light of mine
I'm gonna let it shine
This little light of mine
I'm gonna let it shine
Let it shine, let it shine, let it shine

(*Pastor shakes his head in disbelief*)

Peter: (*Continues to sing*)
Shine all over (name of town)
I'm gonna let it shine
Shine all over (name of town)
I'm gonna let it shine
Shine all over ...

Pastor: (*Interrupts*) Peter, what are you doing?

Peter: Oh, hi, Pastor. You know what I'm doing. In Sunday school last week the teacher said that we should let our lights shine for Jesus so others will see it and let him into their lives. So, that's what I'm doing! (*Shines light into Pastor's eyes*)

Pastor: Now stop that! And turn that thing off! You must not have listened very closely. The teacher did say we should let our lights shine so others will see the change Jesus has made in our lives, but I don't think she meant we should carry around flashlights.

Peter: Well, my mom won't let me play with matches, and I sure can't take a lamp everywhere I go, and ...

Pastor: (*Interrupts*) No, Peter, you still don't get it. Remember when you asked Jesus into your heart?

Peter: Sure, I'll never forget that. He changed my life all around! He forgave me of all my sin and came into my heart to stay, and I'm so glad he's there that I just want to tell everyone!

Pastor: That's it, Peter! All you need to do is tell and show others what Jesus has done for you. That's how you let your light shine — not by shining a flashlight on their faces, but by how your life shines since Jesus came there to stay.

Peter: Oh, I get it, Pastor! My life is the light that should shine, not a flashlight!

Pastor: Yeah! (*Under his breath*) Finally. Remember the verse we learned in Sunday school?

Peter: Sure! Uh ... how does it go?

Pastor: It's Matthew 5:16, where Jesus says, "Let your light shine before men, that they may see your good deeds and praise your Father in Heaven."

Peter: Wow! I like that verse.

Pastor: Me, too. Hey, if you want to sing that song again, I'll sing it with you.

Peter: Okay — but this time I think I'll sing it a little differently now that I understand its meaning. Thanks, Pastor.

Pastor: Oh, you're welcome ... Why don't you boys and girls sing along with us?

(*All sing together "This Little Light Of Mine"*)

"Forgive Us Our Debts"

Peter: The nerve of that guy! Who does he think he is, anyway? Trying to cheat me like that. What a creep!

Pastor: Hi, Peter. I couldn't help overhearing. You sound a little upset.

Peter: Well, I'm not.

Pastor: You're not?

Peter: No — I'm a *lot* upset!

Pastor: Over what?

Peter: Over that rotten Steve, that's what. Do you know what he did to me?

Pastor: No.

Peter: He cheated me, that's what he did. That no-good crook!

Pastor: What did he do?

Peter: What did he do? I'll tell you what he did. He cheated me, that's ...

Pastor: (*Interrupts*) Peter, how did he cheat you?

Peter: He borrowed fifty cents from me last week and said he'd pay me back today. But when today came, did he pay me back? No. He asked me to wait another week! Of all the low-down, crummy, underhanded ...

Pastor: Now, that's terrible!

Peter: Isn't it? If there ever was a messed-up guy who didn't know the right way to treat someone, it's ...

Pastor: (*Interrupts*) It's you, Peter.

Peter: ... It's me, Peter. Huh? Me?

Pastor: That's right. Don't you remember last month when I loaned you two dollars, and you didn't pay me back when you said you would?

Peter: Yeah.

Pastor: I forgave you, didn't I? I didn't make you pay back a cent, did I?

Peter: Ummm, no. You didn't.

Pastor: And yet here you are getting all mad at Steve over an even smaller amount!

Peter: Well, yeah — but this is different.

Pastor: Different how?

Peter: Uh, different 'cause this time it's not me owing the money.

Pastor: Don't you remember our Sunday school lesson on this?

Peter: Not really.

Pastor: It's in the last part of Matthew 18. Something just like this happens, except it's over even more money, and guys get thrown in jail.

Peter: Really?

Pastor: Yes. The lesson is that we can't expect God to forgive us if we won't forgive others. Understand?

Peter: You mean I should forgive Steve?

Pastor: Exactly. Besides, he didn't say he's not going to pay you back ever. Give him the extra week he asked for.

Peter: I guess I could. (*Pauses*) Until then, would you lend me the fifty cents, Pastor?

Pastor: Ummm, Peter ...

Peter: I'm just kidding! I really want to know if you'll come with me to tell Steve that I forgive him for being late.

Pastor: Sure. I'm always eager to lend you my support.

I'm Allergic To That Word "School"

Pastor: Hi, Peter.

Peter: Hi, Pastor.

Pastor: How's school?

Peter: Oh, no! (*Covers ears with hands*)

Pastor: What's the matter with you?

Peter: Don't say that terrible word.

Pastor: What word? School?

Peter: (*Covers ears again*) No, no. Now you've said it again. Can't you see I'm allergic to that word?

Pastor: Oh, Peter. If you're allergic to something, you break out.

Peter: I'd like to break out.

Pastor: You mean you really want to break out?

Peter: Yeah! I'd like to break out of school.

Pastor: Now, Peter, sch ... uh ... you know where, is not that bad.

Peter: Well, it's sure not that good.

Pastor: Now, you know you need to go to ... you know where.

Peter: Not as bad as I need to stay at home.

Pastor: What do you need to do at home?

Peter: *Nothing!* And that's what I do best.

Pastor: Now, you'd get tired of doing nothing.

Peter: Not me. I'd like to do it eight days a week and thirty hours a day. (*Laughs*)

Pastor: God doesn't like for us to be lazy. He tells us in Proverbs what he thinks about idleness. But, I know someone who does like lazy people.

Peter: (*Interested*) Who?

Pastor: The Devil.

Peter: I sure don't want him to like me. He's mean.

Pastor: He's tricky, too. You see, he gets someone to do his dirty work for him.

Peter: What do you mean?

Pastor: He gets us to use our hands for him, if we do bad things. He uses our eyes when we see things we shouldn't. When we go places we shouldn't, he is using our feet, and he uses our ears to hear things we shouldn't hear.

Peter: (*Very quiet, as if thinking, then feels his nose*) Then all I got left is my nose. I'm sure glad he can't use that.

Pastor: Oh, yes, he can.

Peter: How?

Pastor: Well, you see there are young people who sniff glue and other things that are very harmful to them. So, when they do that, the Devil is getting them to use their noses for him, too.

Peter: (*Touches his nose again*) Say, Pastor!

Pastor: What?

Peter: Would you give me a ride to school tomorrow?

Pastor: I sure will, Peter.

God's Phone Number

Pastor: Hello, Peter. What's the matter? You look like you lost your last friend.

Peter: That's the way I feel. I wish I could go out and play, but I have to stay inside until I'm feeling better. I sure do miss my friends.

Pastor: Why don't you try calling them on the phone?

Peter: I tried that.

Pastor: Well, what happened?

Peter: Jerry's line was busy; Freddy wasn't home; and nobody answered at Billy's house.

Pastor: I've got a phone number for you, Peter, and this line is never busy. (*Holds up card*)

Peter: (*Reads card*) Jeremiah 33:3. What kind of phone number is that?

Pastor: That's God's phone number, Peter. In the Bible, God says in Jeremiah 33:3, "Call unto me and I will answer you." Whenever you need a friend, you know you can call on God and he'll listen to you. God does that because he loves us so much.

Peter: Wow, you mean God will be there whenever I want to talk to him?

Pastor: That's right, Peter.

Peter: And I won't get a busy signal? A lot of people must be wanting to talk to God.

Pastor: No, Peter. You won't get a busy signal. God's never too busy to listen to anyone who calls out to him.

Peter: Well, all right! That's one phone number I'm never going to forget — Jeremiah 33:3!

On The Lighter Side

Pastor: Well, Peter, how are you today?

Peter: I'm terrific!

Pastor: By that, do you mean that you are happy?

Peter: Right!

Pastor: That's good, because when you are happy everyone is happy.

Peter: What do you mean by that?

Pastor: Never mind. What have you been up to lately?

Peter: Oh, about eleven o'clock — but I haven't slept for days.

Pastor: Why not?

Peter: 'Cause I sleep nights!

Pastor: Did you take a bath today?

Peter: Why? Is one missing?

Pastor: Of course not, silly. It's just that you look pretty dirty.

Peter: Thank you. I look pretty when I'm clean, too! Say, Pastor, do you exercise?

Pastor: Of course, why do you ask?

Peter: Well, a friend of mine told me about a couple whose doctor said they needed exercise.

Pastor: What did they do?

Peter: The man bought a set of golf clubs.

Pastor: Great. What about the woman?

Peter: The man bought her a lawn mower.

Pastor: Peter, do you have any talent besides telling jokes?

Peter: I'm good at riddles. Try this: Seven cows are walking in a single file. Which one can turn around and say, "I see six pairs of horns"?

Pastor: The first one, of course!

Peter: Wrong! Cows don't talk.

Pastor: Well, I've got something important to talk about today.

Peter: You aren't going to preach, are you?

Pastor: No, today we are going to talk about God's world!

Peter: Where's that at? Is it like Disney Land?

Pastor: No, silly. This world we live in is God's world.

Peter: Hmmmm.

Pastor: Everything was created by God. Jesus told us to look at the lilies ...

Peter: Where? Where?

Pastor: Almost everywhere you look you can see something beautiful that God made.

Peter: Can you eat it?

Pastor: That's the trouble with you, Peter, you're always thinking of your stomach. Look out there. See all those beautiful people?

Peter: Beautiful women, yes. I don't know about the men.

Pastor: God made us all. We are all his creatures, part of his creation. In return, remember that God deserves the best — our love! In the book of Ephesians we are told that we should all be kind, tenderhearted, forgiving one another.

Peter: That's great. I'll try to remember that.

Pastor: Every time you comb your hair, try to think of that verse.

Peter: Who combs their hair?

Pastor: Well, every time you think about your hair, remember God loves you, and be thankful.

Peter: Before we go, I have one last joke.

Pastor: Okay, what is it?

Peter: Two men were walking along the street. One of them said: "Bet you a dollar you can't say The Lord's Prayer." "Of course, I can ... Now I lay me down to sleep ..." "Well, you sure fooled me, here's your dollar."

Pastor: Good-bye, folks. It's been fun being with you.

Peter: Good-bye — God bless you — have a happy day!

Too Old For Heaven

Pastor: Hi, Peter, how are you today?

Peter: Hi. If you must know, I'm in a terrible mood.

Pastor: Why, Peter, what's wrong?

Peter: I was reading my Bible ...

Pastor: (*Interrupts*) And that made you sad?

Peter: Yes, because I'm growing up, Pastor. I won't be a kid much longer.

Pastor: Yesterday you were wishing you were a teenager.

Peter: That's before I started to read Matthew, chapter 18.

Pastor: What did it say?

Peter: It said teenagers can't go to heaven.

Pastor: Really?

Peter: It said you have to be like a little child to go to heaven.

Pastor: Let me read that passage to you again, Peter. "At that time the disciples came to Jesus and asked, 'Who is the greatest in the kingdom of heaven?' He called a child, whom he put among them, and said, 'Truly I tell you, unless you change and become like children, you will never enter the kingdom of heaven.' "

Peter: Well, Pastor, was I right?

Pastor: No, I'm happy to say.

Peter: No? Didn't Jesus say you have to be a little child?

Pastor: Peter, being a child doesn't mean going back to childhood. When you accept Jesus as Savior, you become a child spiritually.

Peter: So, old people can go to heaven? Like you, Pastor?

Pastor: Yes. (*Laughs*)

Peter: Anyone can, if they believe in Jesus?

Pastor: That's right. Now I hope you will stop worrying and get that smile back on your face.

Puzzled

Pastor: (*Trying to play a hand-held computer game*) Now, let's see. If I press this key ... No, that isn't it. Maybe if I ... Awww! I give up!

Peter: Something wrong, Pastor?

Pastor: I should say, Peter. These newfangled gadgets can give an old man dark hair. How in the world do you play this crazy game?

Peter: Let me see. Hmmmm. Looks like it takes some figuring out. Let me have time to play it a bit and maybe I can get the hang of it.

Pastor: There ought to be instruction books for these things.

Peter: I thought when people got to be your age they knew everything.

Pastor: (*Chuckles*) No, I'm afraid not. There are many things people my age don't understand.

Peter: Like what?

Pastor: Well ... uh ... God, for instance. And how God created everything. We know that God created the world, but we don't know how. Did you ever think about how some of the fruit we eat was created?

Peter: Several times, but I had to stop because it drove my head bananas. (*Laughs*) Get it? Fruit? Bananas?

Pastor: You know, Peter, we have a great God. Another thing that I've often tried to figure out is how God has always been.

Peter: Yeah, God has no beginning, does he?

Pastor: That's right! And no ending either. Have you ever tried to imagine eternity?

Peter: Yeah, and the closest I've ever come to experiencing it is when I'm waiting for my fifteen-year-old sister to get ready for church.

Pastor: (*Chuckles*) But there are some things we can understand about God. And there is a book to explain who God is.

Peter: That could only be the Bible, right?

Pastor: Right you are. No other book in the world tells about God like the Bible does.

Peter: That's because the Bible was inspired by God himself.

Pastor: Say, you're pretty smart. Do you think you're smart enough to figure this game out?

Peter: I don't know. But I do know one thing. Without the Bible, I'll never understand God.

"Wait Upon The Lord"

(Today the puppet is wearing the "girl's wig." I call her Petra. On top of her head, she is wearing a paper doily with a ribbon to tie around her head)

Pastor: Good morning, Petra! How are you? I know I shouldn't ask, but what is that silly thing on your head?

Petra: Yes, by all means, you should ask — and it's not silly.

Pastor: Well, pardon me! But you must admit it does look silly. You still didn't tell me what it is. Are you planning on someone setting a piece of cake on your head?

Petra: Now who's being silly? No, that shows that I'm a waitress! You've seen waitresses who sometimes wear little hats ... and I'm a waitress for the Lord!

Pastor: Ooh, now I see! Yes, I think that's great! We should all do our jobs "for the Lord." But say, I didn't know you were a waitress ... Where do you work?

Petra: You never do understand! I don't have a job as a waitress. I'm a waitress for the Lord!

Pastor: Yes, yes, you already said that. I know ... you're just "waiting" to tell me all about it, so go ahead!

Petra: Well, that's better. Do you remember in church last Sunday we read in Isaiah 40:31, "Those who wait for the Lord shall renew their strength ..."? Well, I want to be like that, so I'm going to "wait upon the Lord."

Pastor: ... wait for the Lord? Now, wait a minute! There's that word again! How are you going to serve the Lord his dinner?

Petra: Sometimes I think you don't even try to understand! What a waitress really does is to stand by and be ready to do whatever her master needs done. I guess that's how I want to be with the Lord — standing by, ready and waiting. Now do you see what I mean? That's how I'll serve him.

Pastor: Yes, yes, I do. I guess I never thought of it just like that. Yes, in fact, that's very good. "Those who wait for the Lord shall renew their strength, they shall mount up with wings like eagles, they shall run and not be weary, they shall walk and not faint." ... Yes, Petra, it really does make sense. Now, where can I get one of those little hats?

Petra: Aw, come on, don't tease. I've gotta go now.

Pastor: Hey, wait for me!

"A Star Is Born"

Pastor: Hi, Peter!

Peter: Who is it? Who is it? (*Acts as if he can't see*)

Pastor: It's me — Pastor! What's wrong with you? Why are you blindfolded?

Peter: These are my sunglasses.

Pastor: Well, why are you wearing sunglasses inside?

Peter: Can you keep a secret?

Pastor: (*Whispers*) What's your idea of a secret?

Peter: It's when you only tell one person at a time.

Pastor: Then I can keep a secret. Tell me.

Peter: I'm going to be a movie star, Pastor Baby!

Pastor: That's silly. But why are you blindfolded?

Peter: Sunglasses. We movie stars all wear sunglasses.

Pastor: Why?

Peter: So people won't know us.

Pastor: But I thought movie stars wanted to be known.

Peter: We do. But when we get known, we wear sunglasses so no one will know us.

Pastor: You know, Peter, I think it is smart on your part to wear sunglasses.

Peter: You do?

Pastor: Yes. It covers up part of your face. (*Laughs*)

Peter: You'll see. I'll be famous.

Pastor: As what?

Peter: A singer. I compose songs.

Pastor: Decompose would be more like it. I have some advice for you, Peter. When you sing, breathe through your nose.

Peter: Why?

Pastor: That way you'li keep your mouth shut. (*Pauses*) Peter, have you prayed about this?

Peter: Certainly. I said, "Lord, I want to be a movie star. Make me popular so I can make lots of money."

Pastor: Peter, it's not right to make plans and ask God to bless them.

Peter: It's not?

Pastor: No. We are supposed to seek God's guidance. If we get our plan from God in the first place, it will already be blessed. Does that make sense?

Peter: Well, (*Hesitates*) yeah!

Pastor: That's what we are told in Proverbs 3:6: "In all your ways acknowledge him and he will make straight your paths." Can you say that?

Peter: You mean recite it? I think so. "In all your ways acknowledge him and he will make straight your paths." Hey, Pastor, I changed my mind. Guess what I'm gonna be.

Pastor: I don't know. What?

Peter: A ventriloquist!

Goin' Fishin'

Pastor: (*Calls*) Peter! Peter! Oh, hi, Peter!

Peter: Good morning, Pastor. What's on your mind?

Pastor: I want to know if you would like to go to the park with me. We could fly a kite or something! Isn't that a good idea?

Peter: Uh, yeah, that really does sound like fun, but I've got something important to do ... I'm goin' fishin'! I was on my way when I heard you call.

Pastor: Fishing? Peter, you don't even like fish. You won't eat it when your mom cooks it either. Why would you want to waste a beautiful day by going fishing?

Peter: Oh, Pastor, I wouldn't be wasting my time. Matter of fact, it's one of the best ways I know to spend my time!

Pastor: I don't understand, Peter. Besides, if you were goin' fishin', you'd need a fishing pole and lots of other stuff!

Peter: Pastor, I've got everything I need ... right here in my hand!

Pastor: What do you mean, Peter? You can't carry all that stuff in one hand. You mean you have a fishing pole and a fishing line, and ... Oh, no, Peter ... you couldn't ... ohhhhhh, Peter!

Peter: What, Pastor?

Pastor: You're not carrying worms in your hand, are you? Yecccchhh!

Peter: No, Pastor, I promise you I don't have any worms in my hand. In fact, I don't have any of those things you named in my hand ... No fishin' pole ... no fishin' line, nothing like that!

Pastor: Then how can you catch any fish? You've got to use something.

Peter: You're right ... That's why I have my Bible right here in my hand. I can sure be a *fisherman* with my Bible!

Pastor: Just what kind of fish are you trying to catch?

Peter: I thought you'd guess, Pastor. Jesus said in Matthew 4:19, "Follow me, and I will make you fish for people." That means because I'm a Christian, I want to tell others about Jesus.

Pastor: That's the best kind of fishing, Peter, and your Bible is the right way to catch "people-fish"! It tells all about how Jesus loves us and wants to save us.

Peter: You're right, Pastor. Hey, would you like to go fishin' with me? Fishin' for people?

Pastor: Sure! What are we waiting for? Let's go!

Paul The Pie Maker

Pastor: Well, Peter, how are you getting along in Sunday school?

Peter: Fine. I'm learning a lot.

Pastor: What did you learn today?

Peter: I didn't know before this morning that Paul made pies.

Pastor: What?

Peter: Our teacher was telling us in Sunday school how Paul was a pie maker.

Pastor: Paul wasn't a pie maker.

Peter: I wonder what kind of pies he made?

Pastor: Paul didn't make pies! Paul was a missionary.

Peter: He must have made all kinds of pies.

Pastor: Paul was an apostle; he preached God's Word.

Peter: Yeah, and he made pies in his spare time. I mean he had to do something the rest of the week.

Pastor: He preached and worked for God every day.

Peter: He did? Must not have left much time for pie making.

Pastor: Peter, listen to me!

Peter: I'd like to have eaten one of Paul's pies!

Pastor: Peter! Read my lips! Paul didn't make pies!

Peter: Oh, yes he did, smarty!

Pastor: Peter ...

Peter: You always think you know it all.

Pastor: Peter ...

Peter: Well, I got you this time, 'cause my teacher told me.

Pastor: Peter ...

Peter: She said Paul made pies.

Pastor: Okay, Peter, where does it say that in the Bible?

Peter: Boy, Pastor, I'd think you would know.

Pastor: Peter ...

Peter: It says that "Paul went to fill-a-pie."

Pastor: Fill-a-pie? Paul went to fill-a-pie?

Peter: That's right!

Pastor: Fill-a-pie? Philippi. That's a town, not a pie! Paul went to the town of Philippi. Boy, Peter, you sure got mixed up on that Sunday school lesson.

"The Bread Of Life"

Pastor: Good morning, Peter. How are you today?

Peter: I'm fine, I think. How do I look?

Pastor: Well, you do need a haircut.

Peter: That's what the man at the pool said. He told me, "No one with long hair is allowed in the pool."

Pastor: Oh?

Peter: Yeah! So I told him that many great leaders had long hair.

Pastor: Like who?

Peter: Moses had long hair.

Pastor: What did the man at the pool say then?

Peter: He said, "Don't worry, kid; Moses isn't allowed in our pool either."

Pastor: Well, I have something really important to talk about today.

Peter: And what might that be?

Pastor: Today we're going to talk about food.

Peter: My fa-vo-rite subject. I'll have two cheeseburgers, a hot dog, an order of fries, and ... say, you aren't going to cook it, are you?

Pastor: No. In fact, no one is going to cook it.

Peter: You mean ... it's raw?

Pastor: No, what I mean is, we're going to talk about food, not eat it.

Peter: That's no fun.

Pastor: Oh, yes, it is. Today we are going to talk about the Bread of Life. Do you know where to find the Bread of Life?

Peter: (*Melodically*) At McDonald's?

Pastor: Cut that out. The Bread of Life is found in the Bible.

Peter: You mean that white *goop* that came down from the sky?

Pastor: You are close. The white stuff you are thinking of is not the Bread of Life, though. You are thinking of manna.

Peter: That's a strange name for food.

Pastor: Not really. You see, the Children of Israel had been in a great big wilderness for a long time, and there wasn't anything for them to eat. All the food was gone and they were getting hungry. It looked like they were all going to starve to death.

Peter: Ronald McDonald to the rescue!

Pastor: Cut that out. They didn't have hamburger joints back then.

Peter: So they all kicked the bucket.

Pastor: No, they didn't all kick the ... die! They prayed and asked God to help them, and the next morning when they woke up there was white stuff all over the ground.

Peter: Snow!

Pastor: No, it wasn't snow. They had never seen anything like it before. So they all walked around saying, "Manna, manna."

Peter: Not much for conversation, were they?

Pastor: You missed the point. In their language "manna" means "What is it?"

Peter: I still think I would rather have a hamburger.

Pastor: Wait a minute. I said that manna was not the Bread of Life.

Peter: It wasn't?

Pastor: No, it was just a picture of the *real* Bread of Life.

Peter: Yech! Pictures don't taste good.

Pastor: (*Laughs*) No, what I mean is that the manna represented the true Bread of Life.

Peter: So, what is the true Bread of Life?

Pastor: Stop and think. The manna came down from heaven to earth.

Peter: Yeah.

Pastor: All the children of Israel were empty inside and dying.

Peter: Poor folks.

Pastor: But the manna was sent to fill them up and give them life.

Peter: I'm getting hungry.

Pastor: Come on now, what do you think the manna represented?

Peter: Food

Pastor: Now, Peter, think harder.

Peter: You mean the manna represented Jesus?

Pastor: Very good. So it is Jesus who is the true Bread of Life.

Peter: I think I can see it now.

Pastor: Well, let's look at it again. People today are empty inside if they don't know Jesus. It is their sins that keep them empty and separated from God.

Peter: Does sin cause you to be hungry? 'Cause I'm starving!

Pastor: Sin leaves us spiritually empty inside. People who don't know Jesus are starving for something to fill their lives. Their sin is causing them to starve spiritually.

Peter: But Jesus came down from heaven, so that we could be filled, right?

Pastor: That's right. You see, if the Children of Israel had refused to eat the manna, they would have died. If they let the manna fill them, they could live. If we let Jesus fill our lives, he will give us life and make us to be brand new people. Since I am a Christian, Jesus has changed me. I'm a brand new person. So when I look at myself in a mirror now, do you know what I say?

Peter: Manna, manna — what is it?

Pastor: Say good-bye to the boys and girls.

Peter: Good-bye, boys and girls. Have a great week.

God Hates Lying

Pastor: Good morning, Peter. It's good to have you here this morning.

Peter: It's good to be here, even though I didn't sleep well last night.

Pastor: Oh, what was the matter?

Peter: I plugged my electric blanket into the toaster and kept popping out of bed.

Pastor: Well, I see you're still telling those awful jokes. Tell me, Peter, how come you were running when I saw you last night?

Peter: I was stopping a fight.

Pastor: How could you be stopping a fight when you were running away?

Peter: Because, it was between me and this other guy.

Pastor: Seriously, Peter, you don't look so good. What's the matter?

Peter: Oh, nothing.

Pastor: Well, you sure look like something's wrong.

Peter: Well, if you must know, I just realized I've gotten into a terrible habit.

Pastor: I thought something was wrong.

Peter: I even did it to you just then.

Pastor: You did? What did you do to me?

Peter: I lied to you.

Pastor: You did? I didn't know.

Peter: That's the trouble. Lots of times the person you lie to doesn't know. So, you think you're getting away with it. But you're not, God knows.

Pastor: That's right, God knows everything. But what did you lie to me about?

Peter: I just told you nothing was wrong with me ... and something was.

Pastor: Oh.

Peter: It has become as easy for me to lie as it is to tell the truth.

Pastor: Boy, you do have a bad habit.

Peter: Yeah, and bad habits are a lot easier to make than to break.

Pastor: And lying is a bad habit that's easy to get into, isn't it?

Peter: It sure is, and once you tell a lie it grows.

Pastor: That's right. You have to tell another lie to cover up the first one.

Peter: And another, and another.

Pastor: And God doesn't want us to lie. In fact in the book of Proverbs it says that God hates lying. In Proverbs 6:16-19 it says: "There are ... things the Lord hates ..."; and then it lists seven things including "a lying tongue."

Peter: I always thought God was a God of love.

Pastor: He is, but he hates evil things.

Peter: Then I guess he does hate lying.

Pastor: I guess you do have a problem.

Peter: Can you help me, Pastor? Can you help me stop lying?

Pastor: I don't know. Only God can do that, but you have got to let him.

Peter: How?

Pastor: Well, you made a good start. You know you are sinning when you lie.

Peter: If that's a good start, wow, do I have a good start!

Pastor: Well, I think the next thing you should do is ask God to forgive you for all the lies you have told.

Peter: Okay, what next?

Pastor: Ask God to help you *not* to lie anymore. Ask God to remind you when you are doing it so you can stop before you tell it; or at least before you finish it.

Peter: Okay, but it won't be easy.

Pastor: And then, every time you forget and tell a lie, ask God right then to forgive you.

Peter: Out loud?

Pastor: Well, I don't think that's necessary. But you will want to change your lie to the truth right then. And you will have to do that out loud.

Peter: You mean I have to tell the person I lied to that I lied to them?

Pastor: I guess so. After all, if you're really sorry, you don't want to leave them thinking the lie is the truth, do you?

Peter: Well, no.

Pastor: If you do those things, I bet you'll stop lying in no time.

Peter: Thanks. I'm going to start right now. Oh say, I've got a question. What if somebody asks me something I don't want to tell them. Is it all right to lie then?

Pastor: Of course not. Just tell them the truth. Tell them you don't want to tell them.

Peter: Yeah, I guess I could do that. Well, I guess I'd better be going now. So long, boys and girls. Keep away from the bad habit of lying ... God doesn't like it.

The Memory Verse

Peter: Good morning, Pastor. May I say a memory verse?

Pastor: I didn't know you knew a memory verse, Peter.

Peter: Sure, I learned it in Sunday school.

Pastor: That's neat. Well, let's hear it.

Peter: (*Clears throat*) Teach a ... a ... (*Giggles*) teach a ... old dog new tricks.

Pastor: (*Shakes head*) Ooh, Peter, that's not right. Come on now, try again.

Peter: Okay. Teach a ...

Pastor: (*Softly*) child!

Peter: Don't tell me, I know. Teach a child ... (*Thoughtfully*) teach a child ... some manners.

Pastor: I wish someone would teach you some manners. You said you knew this verse.

Peter: But I do know this verse. I've already said part of it.

Pastor: All right. Let's hear it again.

Peter: Here goes! Teach a child how he should ... how he should ... how he should live, and ... and ... and give him a car. (*Makes a car sound*)

Pastor: Peter, Peter, what's the matter with you?

Peter: Something wrong?

Pastor: Your memory verse is!

Peter: Hey, I just remembered, remember. That's it — remember, remember.

Pastor: Okay, okay, say it.

Peter: (*Clears throat*) Teach a child how he should live, and he will remember ... his memory verse.

Pastor: (*Shakes his head*) I'm sorry, but that's not it. I will say it for you. "Teach a child how he should live, and he will remember it all his life." Proverbs 22:6.

Peter: You know it, too!

Pastor: Yes! Now you say it — right?

Peter: Sure. "Teach a child how he should live, and he will remember it all his life." Proverbs 22:2.

Pastor: Six! Six!

Peter: Proverbs 22:6. (*Pastor sighs in relief. Peter is happy*) How was that, Pastor? I bet you didn't think I knew it.

The Prayer Chain

Pastor: Good morning, Peter!

Peter: Good morning, Pastor! I just had a terrific idea. Do you want to know what it is?

Pastor: Well ... I don't know. Is it going to get us in trouble?

Peter: No. Not unless you tell.

Pastor: It doesn't sound like something that we should be involved in, then.

Peter: Aw, come on. Just listen.

Pastor: Well, here's my first mistake. Let's hear it.

Peter: I think I should join the Prayer Chain.

Pastor: That doesn't sound like trouble. How old do you have to be to join?

Peter: I don't know, but I'm quite mature for my age.

Pastor: That's true, but what made you think about joining the Prayer Chain?

Peter: Well ... (*Looks around*) It's the best source for current information on what's going on in peoples' lives.

Pastor: That's right. If there's a problem, people can call the Prayer Chain, and the people of the church will pray for the need.

Peter: Hey, you missed the point! After someone calls and tells me the problem, I get to call the next person on the list, and everyone else that I think might want to know. The best part is, I will be one of the first to know what's going on, and I will be able to add a few of my own ideas to the story.

Pastor: Wait a minute, Peter. You can't do that.

Peter: And why not?

Pastor: It's just not right! When someone calls the Prayer Chain for support, they want you to write down the request just the way they say it, and read it to the next person on the list. You're not supposed to call whoever you want, and you're definitely not supposed to add your own details. That's just gossiping.

Peter: That's not gossiping; sinners gossip. This is the Christian way of talking about others.

Pastor: No! The Prayer Chain is more than that. It is a big responsibility, and there are certain obligations you must fulfill to join, like no gossiping, repeating the request exactly as you heard it, and most importantly, praying for the person that God's will be done in the situation.

Peter: You're making it sound more like work than fun.

Pastor: At this point, I don't think that you're quite ready to join the Prayer Chain, but you could pray for those who have joined the Prayer Chain.

Peter: Now, there's a terrific idea!

What Do You Want Installed?

Pastor: Today is a very important time for our church as we have the installation service for our Sunday school leaders and teachers for the coming year. At this time I have asked Peter if he would install our educational workers for the coming year ... Peter, I was afraid you were going to be late.

Peter: What's the rush? (*Wears work clothes and carries tools*) What did you want installed? You know I had to get my work clothes on and find my tools.

Pastor: I'm afraid that you misunderstood what we are going to do here. We are going to install our teachers ...

Peter: (*Interrupts*) Just tell me where you want them installed. Maybe we could bolt them up along that wall there. (*Points to a wall with a tool*)

Pastor: But that's not right!

Peter: Okay, if that's not right, then perhaps we might just bolt them to the floor.

Pastor: No!

Peter: Then what would you suggest? We shouldn't install anything along that wall — it's too cluttered as it is ... There aren't any places left to put them ... I know! Let's hang them from the ceiling!

Pastor: (*Gazes at the ceiling and looks horrified*) ... There has been a lack of communication here. Let me explain what we want you to do. (*Gives a brief explanation of the purpose and importance of an installation service*) Do you understand what we want now?

122

Peter: Yes! Now I understand! Why didn't you tell me?

Pastor: Are you sure you understand?

Peter: Yes, positive. (*Holds up a tool*)

Pastor: ... Oh, no!

Peter: In the right hands, these tools can be used to build some very beautiful and useful things. These tools can be used to make something beautiful and functional or something ugly and useless. There is a Master Craftsman, and he can use the tools to make something very wonderful. The leaders and teachers in the Sunday school are like these tools. Wonderful things can be made in our church if we, the tools, will allow ourselves to be placed in the Master's hands. Too often we attempt to do God's work in our own strength and power. We are no more able to do this than a tool is able to make something by itself! Each tool has a different function, and yet all are necessary to fashion any object. In the same manner, each leader and teacher has a different function or job, and all are necessary in the building up of the church.

Pastor: Thank you, Peter. We are all very thankful for our Sunday school teachers and leaders.

Now, boys and girls, as you go back to your seats we are going to have these Sunday school teachers and leaders come forward to be installed.

Weather Or Not

Peter: I can't believe how cold it is today. I read it was so cold in Boston today that the lobsters were throwing themselves into the boiling water.

Pastor: I don't know, Peter. I sort of like it. In a way you could consider this weather as an answer to prayer.

Peter: What do you mean?

Pastor: Don't you remember praying for cooler weather back in July? Well, it finally made it.

Peter: Very funny, Pastor! Very funny! I hate this time of year. My feet are cold, my hands are cold, and snow is all over the place! If this weather keeps up, I think I'll take my extra money and start a "slush fund."

Pastor: Well, I like the weather. It reminds me of God's power and purity.

Peter: I don't get it.

Pastor: Well, God's power is shown through all of the snow here and our human inability to deal with it all. God is in control even though the seasons change.

Peter: Yeah, I see what you mean. The most effective snow removal program we've got is called July.

Pastor: Right! Also, the snow reminds me that God's love for us is pure without blemish or spot, and when we accept Christ as our Savior, we become whiter than snow. We become his chosen people.

Peter: I think you're absolutely right, Pastor. I never thought of it like that. Weather or not, it's great to be one of God's frozen people — I mean *chosen*!

Thankful For Firemen
And Sheriff's Deputies

Pastor: Good morning, Peter. I like your hat. Does that mean you are a Sheriff's Deputy?

Peter: Good morning, Pastor. I like your hat, too. Does that mean you're a Fireman?

Pastor: No! I guess we both know we are wearing these because this morning we are honoring the Firemen and Sheriff's Deputies who serve us in this part of the county.

Peter: That's right! It is our way of saying, "Thank you," for all they do. Say, Pastor, do you know what a back scratcher is?

Pastor: Sure, and in fact I just happen to have one with me this morning. If I get an itch on my back and can't reach it, I just use this handy little gadget.

Peter: Well, do you know why a back scratcher is like a Fireman or Sheriff's Deputy?

Pastor: I give up on that one ... tell me!

Peter: They both lend a helping hand.

Pastor: That's right. I don't know what we would do without them. They risk their lives to keep us safe from fires and criminals.

Peter: We may not all be able to fight fires and arrest criminals, but we can all lend a helping hand when we see people who need help.

Pastor: The Bible teaches us to help one another and to give thanks for people who help us.

Peter: When we hear a siren, we know someone is in trouble and the Firemen and the Deputies are on their way to help.

Pastor: You mean like this: (*Presses hand alarm*) rrrrrrr.

Peter: Where's my motorcycle? ... Here I come to help.

Pastor: As Christians we all need to be alert to hear the sounds of people crying for help. They may not dial 911; they may put on a sad face; or it might be someone crying or someone sulking. Whatever it is that alerts us to the fact that they are in trouble, we should offer our love and try to help.

Peter: Thanks for reminding us, Pastor. And, boys and girls, we are all Deputies of Jesus and Firefighters against the Devil. So, let's always be prepared to help others.

Pastor: Now let us have a prayer together as we thank God for our friends and helpers, the Firemen and Sheriff's Deputies:
    Dear God, this morning we give you special thanks for these brave men and women who risk their lives to help us in fighting fires and keeping law and order in our community. Amen.

Praise God Anyway!

(Peter wears a paper bag over his head)

Pastor: Peter, is that you?

Peter: Nope. Now leave me alone!

Pastor: That is you, Peter! What in the world is wrong with you?

Peter: Everything. That's the problem.

Pastor: What do you mean?

Peter: I just want to disappear for a while, so leave me alone.

Pastor: Oh, Peter, things can't be that bad.

Peter: Oh, yeah? Nothing has gone right since I woke up this morning, so I'm just going to hide here so nothing else can happen to me.

Pastor: Oh, come on. Don't exaggerate!

Peter: Exaggerate nothing! I woke up this morning with a frog in my bed — thanks to my little sister. When I jumped out of bed, I stubbed my toe. Then, as I was hopping around in pain, I tripped on my roller blades, fell, and bumped my head on my chair! Now, does that sound like a great way to start the day?

Pastor: Well, no, not exactly!

Peter: I'll say! And that was just the beginning. I got in trouble on the bus, I got in trouble at school, and I got in trouble at home when my mom found out I had to stay after school!

Pastor: I'm sorry about all that, Peter. It sounds like a great time to praise God.

Peter: Oh, come on! You've got to be kidding!

Pastor: No, I'm serious. No matter how bad things may seem, a Christian can always praise God for lots of things. Just like Psalm 34:1 says, "I will bless the Lord at all times; his praise shall continually be in my mouth." Then, when we start thinking of all the great things God has done for us, we start finding more reasons to praise God.

Peter: Okay, but I can't think of even one praise.

Pastor: Well, you are a Christian, aren't you?

Peter: Yeah.

Pastor: That means that God loved you enough to send his Son to die for you. That makes you pretty special, doesn't it?

Peter: Yeah, I guess you're right. I did do some pretty rotten things today, too. And God still loves me!

Pastor: That's right, Peter!

Peter: Hey, I feel better already. This praise stuff is really great. I'm going to go think of some more praises.

Pastor: Oh, Peter!

Peter: Yeah?

Pastor: Take the bag off your head before you run into something else!

Peter: Oh, yeah! (*Pulls bag off his head*) ... Oh, no, I gave my nose a paper cut!

Pastor: Praise the Lord!

God Watches Over Me!

Pastor: Peter, did you see it rain yesterday?

Peter: Yes, I thought it was the end of the world.

Pastor: Well, it rained hard, but not that hard.

Peter: Huh! It rained so hard at our house that we couldn't see anything in the yard.

Pastor: Yes, but ...

Peter: And the wind blew the rain against the house so hard it sounded like it was going to come through the walls.

Pastor: Well it kinda sounded like ...

Peter: And our front lawn was nothing but a pool of water.

Pastor: Sure, it couldn't run off fast ...

Peter: I just knew God was flooding the earth again.

Pastor: But God promised ...

Peter: I thought the end of the world had come. (*Pauses for Pastor, who says nothing*) Hey, Pastor, aren't you going to say anything?

Pastor: Are you going to let me?

Peter: What do you mean? Sure, I'll let you.

Pastor: Okay. First, God promised never to flood the earth again.

Peter: Oh, I forgot that.

Pastor: That's why we have the rainbow.

Peter: Yeah.

Pastor: And second, it didn't rain that hard anyway.

Peter: Oh, yes, it did! At my house it sure did. You would have thought the world was ending, too, if you had been there!

Pastor: Maybe so. Did you pray?

Peter: No — I was too scared.

Pastor: That's when you need to pray, so God will help you not to be scared.

Peter: You're right. It's just hard to think of that when your mind can't stop thinking of the end of the world.

Pastor: Sure, but doesn't God watch over you all the time?

Peter: Yes.

Pastor: Even in storms?

Peter: Sure!

Pastor: Well?

Peter: God was with me, wasn't he?

Pastor: He sure was.

Peter: I'm glad God looks after us so good.

Pastor: Me, too. Now let's you and me look after getting some lunch!

Becoming A Church Member

Pastor: Hello, there! What's your name?

Peter: Oh, hello, my name is Peter.

Pastor: Well, Peter, why are you here this morning?

Peter: I've come to talk to the kids about church membership.

Pastor: Oh, I see. Are you a member of the church yourself?

Peter: Not exactly.

Pastor: What do you mean, "not exactly"?

Peter: Well, to be a good church member you must be a real person. You see, without your help I couldn't talk or move, but with your help I can tell all the boys and girls about being a church member.

Pastor: Okay then, Peter. What is a church member?

Peter: It is someone who becomes a member of a church! (*Chuckles*)

Pastor: I know that. But how do you become a church member?

Peter: Well, it's like this. There are five basic steps to becoming a church member.

Pastor: What's number one?

Peter: Number one is the most important of them all! You must know Jesus Christ as your personal Savior. When you ask Christ

to come into your heart and forgive you of your sins and you believe that he died, was buried, and rose again for you ... then you
are a Christian and ready to become a church.member.

Pastor: That's very interesting, Peter. What's number two?

Peter: Number two is to be baptized. Jesus was baptized accord-
ing to the Bible, and wants us to share in this experience. To be
baptized is to show all persons what God has already done in your
heart.

Pastor: Good. Now what is number three?

Peter: Number three is to accept the rules and teachings of the
church you become a part of.

Pastor: And number four?

Peter: Number four pertains to stewardship, and that means to
support God's church with your time, talents, and treasure!

Pastor: Wait a minute! You're going too fast! Let me think now ...
number one is to know Jesus as your personal savior, number two
is to be baptized, and number three is to accept the teachings of
my local church.

Peter: So far, so good.

Pastor: Number four is to agree to support God's church with my
time, talent, and treasure. Yes, I think I've got it. What's number
five?

Peter: I have a problem with five.

Pastor: You have a problem with number five?

Peter: Well, you see I only have four fingers and I just ran out of fingers and ...

Pastor: (*Interrupts*) Peter, you may only have four fingers, but you can still give us rule number five.

Peter: Yeah, I suppose so. You kids are lucky to have five fingers! Well, number five is to have the present membership welcome you into the church fellowship. They extend the right hand of fellowship!

Pastor: That's terrific, Peter! You surely have given us something to think about concerning church membership. Thank you for coming this morning!

Peter: You're welcome. I'll see you later. See you later, boys and girls.

Let Somebody Else Do It

Peter: Good morning, Pastor.

Pastor: Good morning, Peter. What's new?

Peter: Well, I've got some good news and some bad news for you.

Pastor: That sounds familiar. Let's have the bad news first, and get it out of the way.

Peter: Well, it's like this. I told you I would do some recruiting for you. You know, help find people to do some of the many jobs that have to be filled in order to do all the work that needs to be done in the church.

Pastor: That sounds like good news to me.

Peter: Wait until you hear what happened. First of all I met Bill, and told him we need him to fill a spot on the Administrative Board. He said, "Well, uh, er ... I'm sorry. I've gotta go. Let somebody else do it." Then I met Suzy, and I said, "Hi, Suzy. I hear you've got a beautiful voice. How about singing in the choir?"

Pastor: And she said...?

Peter: She said: "I'm pretty busy on Wednesdays. Better let somebody else do it." Next I called on Don. I told him: "You're a pretty outgoing guy, Don. How about doing some church visiting sometime?" You know what he told me?

Pastor: I can hardly wait.

Peter: He said: "I have a hard time getting around. An old football injury, you know. Better let somebody else do it."

135

Pastor: Well, I guess you gave up after that.

Peter: Not on your life. I went to see Jane. I said: "Jane, we're a little short-handed in the nursery. How about working in there every other Sunday?"

Pastor: And she said...?

Peter: Get this, she said: "I'm allergic to baby powder. I guess you'll have to get somebody else to do it."

Pastor: And now the good news, I hope.

Peter: That's right. I got this brilliant idea. I asked them all to meet me at the church, and I told them I had some very bad news to share. I said: "There's been a death. Mr. Somebody Else died. When I asked each of you to do a job, you all told me to 'let Somebody Else do it.' Well, now there is no more Somebody Else. You've got to do it."

Pastor: Well, how did they take that?

Peter: They went into a huddle, then they said to me: "We've decided we were wrong. We'll do the jobs you asked us to ... plus whatever else we can. Give us a Volunteer Menu to fill out."
Boys and girls, when you are asked to do something at home or at school or at church, don't try to shift it off onto Somebody Else. God wants you to use your talents, your mind, your skills, your personality for his work. He has a job for Somebody Else, but he also has a job for you; and for you grown-ups, too! Say good-bye to the boys and girls, Pastor.

Pastor: Good-bye, boys and girls, and have a good week.

136

Responsibility

Pastor: Hi, Peter! What are you doing?

Peter: I don't know.

Pastor: You look like you are going somewhere.

Peter: Okay, if you want to be so nosey, I'm running away.

Pastor: Why?

Peter: Because of my mom and dad. All they want me to do is clean up, do the dishes, clean the bathroom, make my bed, dust the house, and a whole lot more! They treat me like a servant! They don't even want me to eat peanut butter sandwiches in my own bedroom!

Pastor: Peter, do you know what you are doing?

Peter: Yeah, running away.

Pastor: Well, not only that, you're running away from responsibility! When you grow up and get married, your wife won't want to sit in a peanut butter sandwich if you leave it on a chair, now will she? Of course not! And when you get a job, your boss will depend on you to live up to your responsibilities.

Peter: But that's so far away. Kids should be allowed to play and watch television and goof off and have fun while they're kids. Work is for grown-ups.

Pastor: How do you think those grown-ups learned to be good workers? By being lazy when they were kids?

Peter: I never thought about that.

Pastor: Their parents must have taught them responsibility when they were young.

Peter: But they tell me to clean up my own room. I ought to be able to keep that how I want it.

Pastor: The Bible says: "Honor your father and your mother." That means to do as they say.

Peter: But they don't love me.

Pastor: You know that's not true!

Peter: If they love me, why do they make me clean up so much?

Pastor: Don't you know your parents are a special gift from God? And it's because they love you that they are teaching you responsibility. Be glad you have dishes to clean and food to put on plates.

Peter: Yeah, I do like to eat ... especially peanut butter sandwiches!

Pastor: You know, Peter, when grown-ups see that you have learned responsibility, they usually give you more privileges, too. You don't always want them to treat you like a little kid, do you?

Peter: I guess you're right, Pastor. Thanks for the advice. I'll go home and tell my parents I'm sorry, and I'll clean up. I'll even clean up the peanut butter sandwich I hid under my bed!

Actions Not Words

Peter: (*Talking on the telephone*) Well, is that so? Same to you, too, Norman.

Pastor: Peter, what are you so mad about?

Peter: That crazy Norman! Boy, he's got some nerve, crazy Norman, calling me that! That crazy ...

Pastor: (*Interrupts*) Now, Peter ...

Peter: (*Continues to ignore Pastor*) Crazy Norm! Ol' stupid Norm! Crazy Norm! Ol' stupid, crazy Norm!

Pastor: (*Firmly interrupts*) Now, Peter, you just hold on. If you don't calm down, you're going to blow a fuse.

Peter: (*Notices Pastor for the first time*) Huh? What did you say, Pastor?

Pastor: I said, you're going to blow a fuse.

Peter: What do I look like, Pastor, a light bulb?

Pastor: Peter, I just meant that if you don't stop being so upset, you're going to make yourself sick.

Peter: You mean like make myself a sandwich?

Pastor: No, Peter. Oh, never mind! What are you mad at Norman for, anyway?

Peter: (*Gets excited again*) He called me a liar!

Pastor: Norman called you that? That doesn't sound like Norman.

139

Peter: Well, it was the same thing.

Pastor: What do you mean, Peter?

Peter: Well, Pastor, I promised Norman that I would go fishing with him tomorrow, but now I can't because I'm going with my dad instead. So when I told Norman, he said that he expected it, and that he never should have believed anything I said. The nerve of that guy!

Pastor: Now, Peter, you stop it. I think Norman was feeling a little disappointed and unloved.

Peter: (*Surprised*) Unloved? Come on, Pastor, that's silly.

Pastor: I don't know, Peter. Remember last week when you promised to go bowling with him, and backed out at the last minute because you were invited to a party?

Peter: But, Pastor, I told him I was sorry.

Pastor: It's not what you say, Peter, but how you say it.

Peter: Look, Pastor, how many ways can I say it? S-o-r-r-y! Sorry!

Pastor: No, Peter, that's not what I mean. The Bible tells us in First Corinthians, chapter 13, that you can speak in the tongues of men and angels, but if you don't have love, you are a noisy gong or a clanging cymbal.

Peter: You mean that just saying I'm sorry isn't enough, and that if I really care about Norm, I'll keep my promises so that I don't have to say I'm sorry.

Pastor: That's right, Peter. But more than that, you were acting selfishly, and the Bible tells us that love does not insist on its own way.

Peter: Pastor, I think I'll go over to Norman's to see if he wants to go with my dad and me in the morning.

Pastor: I'll go with you.

"... And Be Thankful"

Peter: (*Moans*) Oh, I'm so upset. Boys and girls, have you ever been made fun of? Well, I was! I'm so mad! Oh, what a rotten thing to do.

Pastor: What's the matter, Peter?

Peter: Oh, I'm just upset because of something that happened at school. We had tryouts for the Thanksgiving play.

Pastor: Did you try out for a part and then not get it?

Peter: Well, not exactly. I got a part, but it wasn't the one I had in mind. Everyone nominated me for it.

Pastor: What part are you going to play?

Peter: The turkey! All the kids laughed at me. If I could just get my hands on them!

Pastor: Now, Peter, just because they chose you to be the turkey doesn't mean you have to lose your head! Sorry, that was a poor choice of words.

Peter: Well, I guess I should be thankful I have a part in the play at all. Maybe now I can learn about Thanksgiving.

Pastor: You don't know about Thanksgiving?

Peter: Not really.

Pastor: Well, it all began when the Pilgrims met the Indians.

Peter: Was that at the Super Bowl?

Pastor: No, silly! I can see I'm going to have to explain it better. The first Thanksgiving was in 1621.

Peter: No wonder I don't know about it ... that happened before I was born. As a matter of fact, that was ... ten minus one is, carry the four, square root of fourteen, uh ... that was a long time ago!

Pastor: That's right. In fact, it was even before the United States was formed. It happened at Plymouth Colony.

Peter: You mean everybody in the colony owned a Plymouth?

Pastor: No, but a few of the Indians had mustangs. The colony had been through a bad winter. Many people had starved to death. In the fall, a bountiful harvest was reaped, so the governor declared a celebration. All the colonists got together with the neighboring Indians for three days of feasting and recreation.

Peter: Wow! The original pig-out!

Pastor: Many years later, in 1863, Abraham Lincoln officially proclaimed Thanksgiving a national holiday.

Peter: Boy, that's interesting! So I can follow in the footsteps of Abraham Lincoln by being a turkey!

Pastor: Well, sorta. But even more important — you can please God by being thankful. The Bible says: "Let the peace of Christ rule in your hearts, since as members of one body you were called to peace. And be thankful." "Bless the Lord, oh my soul, and forget not all his benefits."

Peter: You're right, Pastor. I should be thankful for being a turkey! It's not an easy part. That reminds me, I'd better practice my lines. (*Starts gobbling*)

Pastor: Sounds good to me! Come on, you turkey!

Brotherhood

Pastor: Hi, Peter!

Peter: Hi, Pastor!

Pastor: You forgot something, Peter.

Peter: I did? Could you tell ... I forgot to brush my teeth? Oh, my ... is it my breath? Do I need Scope?

Pastor: No, Peter. You're all right. You just forgot to be friendly.

Peter: You mean I'm not being friendly? Well, what am I being? Didn't I say, "Hi"?

Pastor: To me, yes. But what about these boys and girls who came down here to visit with us? Your manners, Peter! Have you forgotten.

Peter: Oh, my ... well, oh, me! I wasn't thinking. I mean, I was thinking of something else ... I mean ...

Pastor: Don't get so flustered, Peter. Just say, "Hi," to our friends. That's all it takes.

Peter: (*Shyly*) Hi, friends. I'm really glad to see you. I was so eager to tell Pastor about a new neighbor that I forgot to be polite. Will you please forgive me? Please?

Pastor: What new neighbor, Peter?

Peter: Ling Su, the new little girl who is living with the Brownes.

Pastor: Oh, yes. I've met Ling Su. I like her. She has a nice smile. And she is pleased when I come to see her.

Peter: But she's different!

Pastor: What do you mean, she's different? She has two eyes, two ears, a nose, mouth, and a chin; she walks around on two feet, just like most other people I know.

Peter: Have you noticed her eyes? They're shaped differently.

Pastor: Different from what? I don't know as the shape of them keeps her from seeing anything the rest of us see. In fact, she seems to notice a little more.

Peter: But her hair is so black ... It's almost like night.

Pastor: And Dottie's is so blond, it's almost white, but we never thought of not liking her because of her hair. Peter, you're being ...

Peter: (*Interrupts*) Now just wait, Pastor. She's just different. And you'll have to admit it. Her skin is a different color, too.

Pastor: Yes, it is.

Peter: And she doesn't say her words quite like we do.

Pastor: So what!

Peter: And she likes different food than we do.

Pastor: Peter, Peter! You are being ridiculous.

Peter: How can you say that, Pastor? You're hurting my feelings. I think our friends ought to be our own kind of people.

Pastor: I don't think so, Peter. If you chose only your own kind, you'd be a lonely little boy. Remember, Peter, God made all the people of the world and he loves them all. God sent his only Son, Jesus, to be born in a Hebrew home. But like the song says, "He loves the little children of the world."

Peter: That isn't easy for us to do. How can we?

Pastor: Well, we can pray and ask God to help us. Let's do that right now: Dear God, forgive us when we have been unkind or felt unfriendly toward anybody else. Help us to remember that you made us all and love us all. Amen.

Attitudes

Peter: Boy, oh boy, oh boy, oh boy! Did I have fun this last week! It was sooo groovy! Just ask me. Go ahead, Pastor, ask me. Did I have fun?

Pastor: Oh, Peter!

Peter: I mean it! Ask me, Pastor. I don't mind talking with you about it. Just go ahead and ask me.

Pastor: All right, Peter. Did you have fun?

Peter: Did I have fun? Did I! It was just so much fun you'd have a hard time believing it. You'd really have ...

Pastor: I know. I'd have a hard time believing it. Just what did you do?

Peter: Oh, I played with Bill. We pretended we were in an ancient kingdom. Jim came over. I put on a paper crown, and they pretended I was an enchanted prince upon whom some wicked witch had cast a spell.

Pastor: Fun, huh?

Peter: Yes ... for a while. Then guess what happened? Sam came over.

Pastor: That was good. You know, "the more the merrier!"

Peter: No, it wasn't good. Bill and Jim were real nice until Sam came over, and then they weren't nice at all.

Pastor: No?

147

Peter: No, they weren't. They whispered to each other and giggled. They left Sam standing by himself looking sad and lonely.

Pastor: It's not much fun to be left out.

Peter: No, it isn't. They said some unkind things and Sam looked sadder and sadder. Tears started rolling down his cheeks and he ran over and pushed over the table we were using as our castle.

Pastor: Wow! I can't believe it!

Peter: It happened, all right. If I'd been two inches closer to that table I wouldn't be here this morning.

Pastor: Narrow escape?

Peter: Too close for comfort.

Pastor: Then what happened?

Peter: I was so scared! Everybody was pretty upset and Sam went home.

Pastor: A fine way to end a "kingdom."

Peter: A bad way to treat a friend! Bill's mother heard the noise and came to see what the trouble was.

Pastor: I suppose she punished Bill?

Peter: Not that time. At least Bill and Jim told the truth, and that helped a lot. They said we were having so much fun that they didn't want anybody else coming in.

Pastor: Then what happened?

Peter: She helped them to see how they would feel if they had been Sam — lonely, wanting to play, being left out, and feeling not wanted. They realized they would have been angry, too. So, you know what they did?

Pastor: What?

Peter: They fixed the table back up. Made an even nicer castle. Then they made some peanut butter and jelly sandwiches and Kool-Aid. Then they went to get Sam.

Pastor: What did Sam say when he saw them?

Peter: I don't know. I just stayed in my chair and pretended to be the enchanted prince.

Pastor: Well, I wonder what happened?

Peter: Oh, I can tell you that. In just a few minutes, they came running back. All three of them, and we gobbled up the sandwiches.

Pastor: I think Bill's mother helped all of you to grow up a little bit on the inside when she talked to you. She helped you remember, "A friend loveth at all times." We all need to grow just as much on the inside by forming good habits and good attitudes as we grow tall and strong on the outside. Then when next fall comes ...

Peter: And people say, "My, how you've grown!" I can think, "I've grown in ways you can't see, too."

Pastor: You will have grown in ways that make you a finer person and a better follower of Jesus.

Stubborn

Peter: (*Chants*) School's out! School's out! Teacher's turned her ...

Pastor: (*Interrupts quickly*) Peter!

Peter: ... boys and girls out.

Pastor: All right.

Peter: Why couldn't I sing, "Teacher's turned her mules out"? Sounds all right to me.

Pastor: Well, sure. It's all right to call a mule a mule, but you're talking about boys and girls.

Peter: Don't boys and girls like to be called mules?

Pastor: Well, do you, boys and girls?

(*Children respond*)

Peter: I wonder why?

Pastor: It's because people usually think of mules as being stubborn and when you call somebody a mule, that's the same as saying he's stubborn.

Peter: Stubborn?

Pastor: Sure. Always wanting his way, determined to have it, refusing to see how the situation looks through the eyes of others. In fact, people who are stubborn are selfish.

Peter: Selfish? Now wait a minute, Pastor. You may be able to accuse me of being stubborn, but you know I'm not selfish. I'd share my last mouthful of pizza with anybody who needed it.

Pastor: Of course you would, Peter. You're good about sharing your stuff, but what about letting others have their way about things part of the time?

Peter: Give me a "for instance."

Pastor: All right. For instance, Joe really likes to play baseball and you don't care much about baseball. You'd rather play football.

Peter: Yeah. I'm a good kicker!

Pastor: So ... you've played football for three days in a row.

Peter: When? Pastor, when?

Pastor: Never mind when. This is a "for instance."

Peter: All right. We've played football for three days and I really looked good. Right?

Pastor: Right! But Joe didn't look so good. Remember, football isn't his thing.

Peter: But he played with me, anyway. Good old Joe! I believe he's getting much better at it, too.

Pastor: Sure, he's a good sport!

Peter: Look at it this way, Pastor. If he keeps on playing and keeps getting better at it, he'll get so he'll really like it. See what I'm doing for Joe. I'm really good for him.

Pastor: That's one way to look at it. Another way is that you've done what you really like to do for three days and now it's Joe's turn to do what he would like to do ... and your turn to do it with him.

Peter: But, I don't like baseball. It hurts my teeth.

Pastor: That's because you haven't learned to catch. Remember what you said, Peter. The more you play, the better you'll get. And the better you get, the more you'll like it!

Peter: I don't want to like it. It's a stupid game.

Pastor: Well, if you don't let others have their way part of the time, and if you don't do it cheerfully, you're being ...

Peter: (*Interrupts*) I know. I'm being stubborn. Ugh! I don't want to be stubborn. I'll play baseball with him. Ugh!

Pastor: But will you do it cheerfully?

Peter: You say I have to be cheerful when I give in?

Pastor: Of course.

Peter: That's asking too much. I can't do that.

Pastor: Was Joe cheerful when he played football?

Peter: Sure. That's what made it fun. I wouldn't have enjoyed playing with him if he had been grumpy.

Pastor: All right, Peter. Then what's going to make you be cheerful when you play baseball with him?

Peter: Hmmmmm ... well, I'm going to remember how much I like Joe. I'm going to remember how he played football with me when he'd rather play baseball. Say, Pastor, you know something?

Pastor: What?

Peter: Joe cares abut me. That's why he hasn't been stubborn. Why, being stubborn is really being selfish.

Pastor: You think so, Peter? Well, you just discovered something really neat. Something you need to think about. Boys and girls, you'll think about it, too, won't you, friends? Bye, now.

Thanksgiving

Peter: (*Sings to the tune of "Up On The Housetop"*)
Out in the kitchen, we start our day,
Preparing for Thanksgiving the usual way.
Turkey and dressing and pies, quite a few,
A-making and a-baking, there's so much to do,

Gobble, gobble, gobble, who wouldn't wobble?
Gobble, gobble, gobble, who wouldn't wobble?
Eating the turkey and all that stuff.
Cleaning up our plates, like we couldn't get enough.

Pastor: "Gobble, gobble, gobble, who wouldn't wobble"? Is that all you think about — food?

Peter: Why not? It's Thanksgiving, isn't it?

Pastor: Sure, it's Thanksgiving. But Thanksgiving is more than cooking all day and then sitting down to a big dinner.

Peter: Yeah, there's all that leftover turkey for days after!

Pastor: You know, Peter, Thanksgiving is a special day set aside for giving thanks.

Peter: Well, I am thankful we can have such a nice dinner.

Pastor: There are many more things we should be thankful for — like our family and all our friends.

Peter: And that new girl in my class at school! (*Sighs*)

Pastor: Yes, and the home we have and our church family.

Peter: I'm thankful for prayer and the Bible.

Pastor: I'm thankful for those who believe in Jesus and really know his love.

Peter: And I'm thankful for the country he has given us to live in, and the way we are free to worship God.

Pastor: I'm thankful for the time it stopped raining in time for the church picnic.

Peter: I'm thankful for other things, too. Like when I got to go to church camp last summer.

Pastor: There is so much to be thankful for, it is good to set aside some time just to think of it all and be thankful.

Peter: You know, Pastor, another thing I'm thankful for?

Pastor: What?

Peter: That when you come to our house for Thanksgiving dinner, you promised to help me with the dishes.

A Thanksgiving Game

Pastor: When you think about Thanksgiving, Peter, what comes to mind?

Peter: Turkey, dressing, and pumpkin pie!

Pastor: Do you think of anything else?

Peter: Well, I suppose I think about things I'm thankful for.

Pastor: That's really what Thanksgiving is all about, you know.

Peter: My teacher plays a game with us at Thanksgiving time. It's the color game.

Pastor: How do you play the color game?

Peter: She picks a color and then everybody in the room thinks of something that color that we are thankful for. Then we go around the room saying what it is.

Pastor: That sounds like fun. Why don't we play? Are you ready? Here's the first color ... Blue.

Peter: The deep blue sea, and the blue sky.

Pastor: How about blue jeans. Boy, I couldn't live without my blue jeans.

Peter: Let's try another color ... Green.

Pastor: My green shirt. It goes so nice with my blue jeans.

Peter: I'm thankful for green grass and trees. Without them we wouldn't have nice, soft grass to play and lay on, or trees to hang swings in.

Pastor: Let's think of things we are thankful for that are yellow.

Peter: I guess I would have to say the sun. Without it we wouldn't be warm, have daylight, and things wouldn't grow.

Pastor: I like butter. I love it on hot blueberry muffins — mmmm!

Peter: This is really a good game. I want to play it with my mom and dad tonight at supper.

Pastor: That sounds like a good idea.

Peter: Boys and girls, when you go home, ask your mom and dad if you can play the color game with them. Then think of all the things you have to be thankful for!

Angels Look At Christmas

Peter: (*Dressed like an angel*) Look at all those people out there! They look like they've had too much to eat!

Pastor: That's because they recently celebrated Thanksgiving, and probably all of them ate too much!

Peter: You mean they only celebrate Thanksgiving one day a year?

Pastor: Yes, just on Thanksgiving Day.

Peter: But shouldn't they give thanks every day? Angels do!

Pastor: People aren't like angels.

Peter: I noticed that. Do you know I heard people talking about Christmas, and they were griping and complaining?

Pastor: I know. You hear them complaining about all the work they have to do to get ready for Christmas.

Peter: Yes, but why would they have to get ready for Christmas? They should have Christmas in their hearts all year.

Pastor: Maybe they don't know about Jesus!

Peter: Why would they celebrate Christmas if they don't know about Jesus? Christmas is Jesus' birthday.

Pastor: I know, but I don't believe some people know what Christmas is. I've heard some people say they dreaded Christmas!

Peter: Dreaded Christmas? But Christmas is such a wonderful time.

Pastor: And people complain about decorating for Christmas. That's what decorations are for — to honor Jesus.

Peter: I guess they don't know about Jesus!

Pastor: You're right! I heard some people say they were going to fight the crowds to shop for Christmas.

Peter: Shop for Christmas? But Christmas isn't something you shop for — it's in your heart!

Pastor: They buy gifts for each other.

Peter: Oh, how nice! Jesus would like that.

Pastor: Yes, except look at them. They don't look happy about giving gifts. Jesus wouldn't like their attitude.

Peter: No, giving should be done with a cheerful heart. Remember how happy the Wise Men were when they brought gifts to the Baby Jesus?

Pastor: Oh, Peter, what can we do to help those people know what Christmas really is?

Peter: I don't know ... I don't know ... Maybe if we just keep on shining for Jesus, someone will look at us and see a shiny star and remember that first Christmas many years ago!

Pastor: That's a good idea. If we will be shiny stars maybe we can help someone find Jesus this Christmas! Boys and girls, will you be Shining Stars for Jesus this Advent Season?

How Do You Catch
The Christmas Spirit?

Peter: (*Carries a butterfly net*) I think I almost had some that time. (*Tries again*) It shouldn't be that hard to catch it. Everybody says there's a lot of it around this time of year ... Sure would be easier if I knew what it looked like.

Pastor: Peter, what in the world are you doing? Have you started taking ballet lessons?

Peter: Of course not, Pastor! I'm just trying to catch some Christmas spirit. Do you know exactly what it looks like?

Pastor: (*Chuckles*) Oh, Peter, you can't catch the Christmas spirit with a butterfly net. It's something that you get inside of you.

Peter: I see ... well, why don't you sneeze on me?

Pastor: Do what?

Peter: If I have to get it inside of me, it must be something you catch like a cold. Come on, Pastor, sneeze on me! Say — maybe you don't have it either.

Pastor: Oh, yes, I do, Peter. I'm so full of it I can hardly stand it, but I didn't get it by being sneezed on.

Peter: Well, how did you get it?

Pastor: The first thing I did was to read about Jesus' birth in the Bible and why God sent his Son to earth as a little baby. I found out the real reason for Christmas is that God loves us so much he sent this Son, Jesus, to save us. Then I had to tell someone else about it. I just couldn't keep it all to myself. When you realize how much God loves us, you just have to love other people, and all the things you do at Christmastime, like buying gifts for your family and friends and fixing baskets of toys and food for poor folks, is just God's love spilling out of you to everyone. That's really the spirit of Christmas, Peter.

Peter: Wow, that's great, Pastor! I'm gonna go home and get my Bible and get started on receiving my share of the spirit of Christmas. Thanks a lot ... and ... Merry Christmas!

Pastor: Merry Christmas, Peter. I think you're getting the Christmas spirit and you will have the best Christmas you ever had.

Boys and girls, remember the real reason for Christmas is to celebrate God's love in the gift of his Son, Jesus — then you, too, will have the Christmas spirit.

An Interview With Santa

(Peter is dressed with a Santa hat and a white beard)

Pastor: Today we have a very special guest who has come a long way to be with us. Let's give a big welcome to Santa Claus.

Peter: Merry Christmas, everyone! After my long, hard trip, it sure is good to be here.

Pastor: I can understand the trip being long, but what made it so hard? Was the weather bad?

Peter: No, it's just that I don't have any feet! But this one kind person gave me a hand.

Pastor: What brings you to this part of the country, Santa?

Peter: This is where I was sewn up, and I just thought it would be good to visit the old hometown.

Pastor: You mean you come from (name of your town)?

Peter: Yes. It's a little-known fact, but nevertheless true.

Pastor: So, how do you find time to come back here during your busiest time of the year? You must be run off your feet right now.

Peter: I told you, I don't have any feet. But you see, I always feel that it's important to take time to stop and reflect on the meaning of Christmas, and I always do that best here.

Pastor: What do you mean?

Peter: As you know, my job is very specialized, and people watch me all Christmas long to see what I'm going to give them. Do you know why I give presents to everyone?

Pastor: I suppose it's because you're such a jolly old fellow.

Peter: I haven't always been this way. I used to be a mean, old grouch. I didn't like anyone.

Pastor: I can't believe that. You were a grouch?

Peter: Yep. It's true.

Pastor: Then how did you ever get to be so jolly, much less give gifts to everyone?

Peter: A very special person and I became acquainted, and you know, he changed me.

Pastor: I thought you were special, but he must have been super special to have done that.

Peter: He is. That's how I got this job.

Pastor: You mean he gave you this job, too?

Peter: Not exactly. I help celebrate his birthday every year by giving gifts to people. It reminds me of the precious gift he gave to me.

Pastor: A precious gift? What did he give you?

Peter: A new life. He took away my grumpy nature, and gave me a deep love for people. I have a purpose in life now — to serve him and to grow to be a better person, and I know I will spend eternity with him.

Pastor: Who is this man? I'd like to meet him, too.

Peter: It's Jesus, and you can know him by simply praying and asking him to come into your life.

Pastor: It's that easy, huh?

Peter: It sure is. And let me tell you, it is exciting growing and getting to know him better. I can't imagine my life without Jesus as a friend.

Pastor: Thank you, Santa, for sharing this with us.

Peter: It was a pleasure. I've got to fly now, or I'll get behind in my job. Good-bye, boys and girls. Don't forget that it's because of Jesus' gift to us that I give you presents, and you give presents to each other. Merry Christmas!

Pastor: Good-bye, Santa. Thanks again for coming.

We Can Give Something To Jesus

Pastor: Hi, Peter! What's the matter with you? I thought you caught the Christmas spirit. It's almost Christmas, and children are supposed to be happy.

Peter: Yeah, I know it. But I don't feel happy.

Pastor: Why not? Is something wrong? Aren't you going to get any presents?

Peter: Sure I'm going to get presents. I always do.

Pastor: What are you so sad about, then?

Peter: Well, I've been thinking.

Pastor: Yes?

Peter: Yes. I'm getting old enough to give some presents this year, and ...

Pastor: So, why don't you give some then?

Peter: Well, I've made presents for nearly everybody. And I've bought a few.

Pastor: Did you get one for, well, ah, well, for ...

Peter: Oh, silly. Of course, I got one for you!

Pastor: Well, I don't see anything to be sad about then.

Peter: Here's my problem. I have a present for people like you, my mom and pop, but Christmas is Jesus' birthday, and I don't know how to give him a present.

Pastor: Well, that isn't as difficult as you think. I remember a Bible verse in Matthew 25 that says: "Just as you did it to one of the least of these who are members of my family, you did it to me."

Peter: Fine, but how can that help me to know how to give Jesus a Christmas present?

Pastor: Well, we can't give Jesus anything personally, like a tie or chocolate, but this verse says we don't have to give anything to him personally.

Peter: I don't know what you're talking about.

Pastor: It means that when you give something to somebody who needs it, it's just like giving it to Jesus.

Peter: That makes sense, all right. But how can I find someone who needs something?

Pastor: How about your little sister? You can help take care of her when your mother is busy shopping or something.

Peter: Do you mean that would be doing something for Jesus?

Pastor: Sure!

Peter: I can think of lots of presents to give Jesus then. I can help with the dishes; I can empty the trash; I can take a gift to Sunday school for the Spanish mission.

Pastor: Now you've got the right idea.

Peter: And you know what? I can give something to Jesus all year, not just at Christmas. I can help people all year long.

Pastor: That's right, and you can even help me sometimes. Boys and girls, this Christmas and all year long, will you remember to give something to Jesus by helping others?

Let's have a little prayer together: O God, we thank you for showing your love to us in the Baby Jesus. Help us to show our love for you by helping others. Amen.

www.ingramcontent.com/pod-product-compliance
Lightning Source LLC
Chambersburg PA
CBHW060800110426

42739CB00032BA/2302

* 9 7 8 0 7 8 8 0 2 3 0 0 2 *